Robert W Hc

A forgotten Loc

By C.L.Hook

Picture Credits:

Chapter one: Sandbanks around Lowestoft.
Chapter one: Robert Hook postcard by H Jenkins.
Chapter Three: John Mewse postcard by H Jenkins.
Chapter Three: Pier Head, Lowestoft postcard by Valentine.
Chapter Three: In the nick of time, postcard Whitefriars press
Chapter Three: The Shamrock, London Illustrated News 1859.
Chapter Three: Lifeboat medal, Player's Cigarettes.
Chapter Three: Nathaniel Colby, London Illustrated News.
Chapter Three: Cork lifejacket, Lowestoft Journal 1886.
Chapter Three: Lowestoft regatta, London Illustrated News.
Chapter Three: Life Saving Apparatus, London Illustrated.
Chapter Three: Sinking of collier, London Illustrated News.
Chapter Three: Dreadnought postcard, Mr Hook collection.
Chapter Three: Norfolk & Suffolk Lifeboat Types, Oxo cubes.
Chapter Three: Black Saturday, London illustrated News 1882
Chapter Three: Robert Hook postcard, H Jenkins.
Chapter Three: Fisheries Expo, London illustrated News 1883.

Special thanks to Archant, P Jenkins, Lowestoft Maritime Museum, Lowestoft Hertiage Centre, British Newspaper archive, John Holmes and the RNLI for their help in writing this book.

Printed by Book Printing UK
Front Cover: Robert W Hook, The John Holmes collection.
Rear Cover: The Old Beach Company Shed.

Foreword

This biography you are about to read has taken months of painstaking research, and without the help of the Lowestoft Heritage Centre and the RNLI it would have been impossible to write. Please don't forget that all the rescues in which Robert Hook, took part were a team effort, and we shouldn't forget the rest of the crew of the Lifeboat or the Old Company men and other beach-men who were involved in the 600 souls Robert Hook rescued. I grew up hearing these following stories from my Grandad, and as a ten-year-old boy, there was nothing better than getting another nautical tale of my first cousin 6x removed before bedtime to get me off to sleep. As a ten-year-old boy my first school trip to the Maritime Museum was the first ever time I saw his picture, and at that point he became my childhood hero and role model.

I'm not the only descendent of Roberts fathers father, there are many of his great great nephews and nieces still going in Lowestoft and in fact after doing the family tree there are descendants all over the world. I can say in all honesty that all the living descendants of Robert in Lowestoft all keep his memory alive in different ways, for example one niece in Oulton Broad even has an oil painting of the first picture in this book on the front cover.

Just before you get started reading the book here is a few explanations of a few of the uncommon words we don't hear anymore; Coxswain (The steersman/senior officer), Galloping

Tom (Fast pace of water), Brig/Brigantine (two-mast sailing ship), Schooner (Two-mast sailing ship, front mast being smaller than the rear), Sloop (A small single mast vessel), Barque (A sailing ship with the rear mast with a sail front and back and the front mast square rigged). Yawl (A two mast sailing boat-four or six oars). Gig (Rowing boat). Salvor (A person or ship making or assisting in salvage). I think that's the main terms which crop up the most, but just in case have a dictionary standing by, So I hope you enjoy reading about the interesting and funny life of Robert Hook., A Coxswain, A Beach-man, A Landlord and A true local forgotten Hero of Lowestoft.

Robert was described in the press as a huge man, vast beard and quick to anger but who inspired the crew and was a man of courage; a courage that is reflected in the fact that he was involved in the rescue of over 600 lives throughout his career, both with the RNLI and the Old Company.

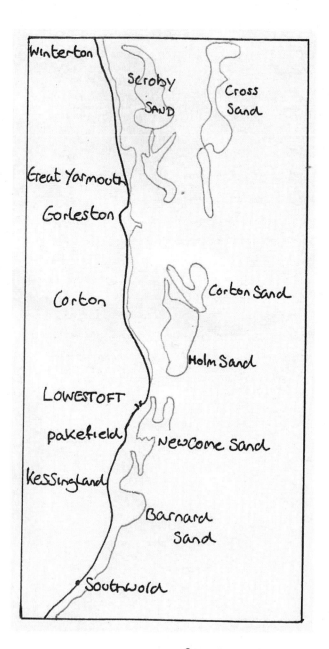

This book is dedicated to my father,

The present

Robert Hook and the Memory of my late sister

Jade Louise Cullen.

Chapter One

A Record of Brave Deeds

This First chapter is the true Autobiography written by Robert Hook for the Lowestoft journal and published in the September 11th edition of 1886 and is as follows;

Within every locality we are almost sure to find what may be termed "representative characters" some, we are sorry to say, no great blessing to themselves or others; while others can prove by a long series of useful efforts for the benefit of their fellow creatures that could have been ill-spared the position they have occupied, and the special work they have undertaken. To this category belong those who have devoted themselves more or less to the duty of saving life and property, or it may be protecting both were they may unwittingly or designedly have been at stake. Such, for instance, are our soldiers, policemen, members of the fire brigades, and last but no means least, our lifeboat crews, the latter of whom are ever ready at the exposed portion of our lengthened coast line to encounter the fury of the elements in carrying out their merciful work.

Many have been the instances of noble heroism our fire brigades have displayed in battling with the devouring element, to the fury of which they have been exposed; and the grand results they have accomplished which thus engaged, and the records of lives of such men as Braidwood and Shaw, the noted chiefs of the London Fire establishments, with those under them, are such as make Englishmen proud of such noble fellows, who count not on their own safety as worth considering while the very existence of their fellow-creatures hang in the balance.

As a rule, the area with which these brave fellows have to deal, and the work they have to do, is generally of a circumscribed character, and though for the time being all their powers must be taxed, and great dangers encountered, yet provision can frequently be made to lessen the dangers to which they are exposed, and circumstances arise may pretty well ensure their own personal safety, and it is only very occasionally we hear of loss of life among them in the discharge of their onerous and praise-worthy duties.

Far different, however, is the character of the work done by our lifeboat crews, and the position they occupy in their noble enterprise. In this respect they have to deal with two of the most fickle and uncertain elements, the wind and waves, and until the men are safe on shore again nothing but uncertainty can be entertained respecting them. To the philanthropic mind the knowledge that we have men all around our exposed coasts ever ready to come and save the "distressed mariners of all nations" is peculiarly grateful, and no wonder need be experienced that the institution under which they work is so generally well supported.

Since the year 1809 this locality has had its lifeboat station, either in connection with the Suffolk Humane Society or the Royal National Lifeboat Institution, and during its existence several hundred lives have been saved by the efforts thus put forth. In order to have any service properly carried out there must be a head, and in this branch that position is occupied by a coxswain to whom is delegated the management of the boat and the ordering of the crew, and the office is regarded as a particularly honourable one among "those who are connected with the service, and brave fellows indeed are most of those who have undertaken its duties.

Among those in this locality, who have held the office, none have had a more lengthened term, or, perhaps, have done nobler work, than the one whose name is Robert William Hook, and whose career is as follows in his own words. And when we say that, though he had temporarily withdrawn from his position, his heart is as responsive as ever to the needs of his fellow-creatures, and he is as ready and as willing as ever to undertake any work of the kind that may be required at his hands, and we feel persuaded nothing more need be stated to show his character than a simple record, from his own lips, of some of these "naval battles" in which he has thus been engaged.

"I was born on the 4th June 1828, and am therefore just over 58 years old. My father was Robert Hook, a fisherman and beach-man, who died a few years ago, aged 88. My grandfather was 87 years old when he died in 1844, and both had been long connected with the service one way or other. My grandfather, as long back as 1804, had a silver medal given him for his services, and on one occasion he pulled off his flannel shirt to wrap round a child, which saved its life. His gravestone is in the churchyard with a record of what he did in this line. When my father joined the service Lowestoft was but a fishing village, and for many years afterwards. The first boat on which I was engaged was the Frances Ann, and she did some good work. I remember when we took a crew out of the Newcastle trader, the Bigwell, in 1848, which got on the Holm Sand, when, beside a crew of 12 or 13, there was a Quaker and Quakeress on board. She knocked off the sand, and soon after we took them on board she sunk in the roadstead.

From my boyhood I have always had a hankering after the work. I was appointed coxswain when Captain Joachin, R.N. (Ah, he was a good man) was superintendent of the station. The first vessel I went to after my appointment was the brig Mary Young of Shields, over 30 years since. She was riding in the roads, and drove up under the Newcome in a gale from the N.E, and knocked her rudder off. She put her "Union" flag downwards to show she was in deep distress. We launched the life boat, and took the crew off, ten in number, and landed them on Kirkley beach. The weather afterwards moderated and we then went and saved the ship as well, because you see we sometimes helped in that work as well as saving life.

The next vessel that I can remember was the Shamrock (s.s), of Dublin, with a crew of 14 hands. She got on Holm Sand on All Saints Day (1st November), 1860, with a strong gale from the S.W. That was hard work, and the ship was lost. Then there was the Lord Douglas, of Dundee, which got on Corton patch, laden with iron. There was a crew of five hands, which we took out. That ship was lost, and the same day there was the silver, of Dundee, with a cargo of iron and bottles. She grounded on Holm Sand, and a crew of four, whom we saved too. This ship was also lost. After this I remember the brig Queen of the Tyne, from shields, coal-laden, which got on a part of Corton Patch we call "Galloping Tom" (that, you know, is because it is dangerous and soon sucks vessels down).

It was before daylight in early spring, the weather thick with rain, and a gale from the S S.W. We were gone some considerable time, and sighted her in the dark. The tide being "done," we let go the anchor to windward of her, and there not being tide enough to take us down, we were compelled to pull it up and let go to the leeward, and were up to the vessel, when we found her lying on the port side with head to the eastward. We picked off eight men from the main-top gallant yard, and the remainder dropped off 10ft, or 11ft. At the time we were lying in a dangerous position, and just as we were hauling away, and after cutting our rigging to let our mast go, I was pulled overboard by the maintop gallant brace. As I was swung round I got hold of the rope, and so was saved.

One of the most exciting affairs, however, we were engaged in, was that of the Osip, of Flume, a brig, laden with maize, which I went to on January 13th, 1866. When she got on the sand the weather was fine, but an S. S.W. gale sprang up. There was a pilot on board of the name of Bailey, from

13

St.Mawes, Falmouth and she was bound from Falmouth to
Hull. The small yawl went to her first, but afterwards
signalled for a larger. The wind and sea, however, increasing,
the lifeboat was signalled for, which was launched
immediately. We were taken in tow by the Rainbow tug,
Captain Porter aboard. When we had got into position the
tug let go of the life boat, and we let go an anchor; but the
wind and sea had increased we were driven to the leeward of
the ship, so that we could get no communication with her.
We thought it best to put a buoy on the cable and set sail,
and go into the roads, and for the Rainbow to tow us home
and get another anchor and cable. Both the brigs' masts were
gone at the time, the crew being made fast by a rope to a
piece of wreck. The ship's deck was out also at the time. We
reached the wreck again in the afternoon time. We went into
the sea, and let go our anchor close to the wreck; and we
then succeeded in getting seven alive, beside the pilot, who
was only just breathing, but he expired while in the boat
from injuries he had received on his head, which was almost
knocked in. Four of the crew, however, were washed off, and
we saw no more of them. This was the day, too, that the new
Gorleston Lifeboat was capsized to the north of Yarmouth
Piers, and 13 out of 16 of the crew found a watery grave. We
had a bottle of brandy put aboard the lifeboat, and
Mr.F.S.Worthington had come out the tug, and had brought
a bottle also, as the poor fellows were quite exhausted. We
got back soon after five o'clock, and had been at it from ten
o'clock in the morning, and the poor men at once taken to
the Sailors Home, where every attention was paid them. Yes,

there was indeed a lot of excitement when we came in, the whole town almost coming down to see us.

The next affair I had to deal with was that of the barque Matilda, from Marseilles to Yarmouth, with oil cake. She struck on Corton Patch in the winter time. It was blowing a gale from the E.N.E. at the time. The vessel struck only two or three times before she fell down in the water, with her mast gone. There was a report came that there was a vessel on the patch, and we launched the life boat, we were towed there by the powerful tug, and were; afloat a considerable time before we were able to get there. We found a portion of the wreck with four men sitting on it, and succeeded in rescuing the whole, though much exhausted. Some of the crew had got into their little boat and drifted over the sand, and made the report. The piece of wreck afterwards came ashore, and was purchased for £6, and the captain took a piece of the "trundle" that he hung to by which his life was saved, and would not part with it for any money. His name was Captain Hanson. That was 22 or 23 years ago.

In 1872 while our crew went to render assistance to the Expedite, of Droback, a Norwegian vessel, one of them broke his leg. The vessel got on the Holm Sand in a N.E. gale. There was a deal of a sea, and the life boat (the Letitia) ran into the sea to get a communication with the vessel, her masts being both gone. Another life boat had been there before we got to the wreck, but didn't go near. We let go the anchor, wore down, and took eight men out, who had been on the wreck several hours, in almost exhausted condition. We ran over the sand and landed them in the harbour, and took them to the Sailor's Home.

Beside these I have assisted in saving many other crews and vessels, almost too numerous to mention. There were 11 hands taken off the Saucy Lass, and five out of the Whim Pilot cutter, of Yarmouth, at the same time. There was the Oswald brig riding in the roads 20 years since. She broke adrift and went ashore. Rescued that crew. I picked up two crews at sea, one on the Northumberland coast, and the other on our own.

The Medora Sawover, of Yarmouth, got on the Newcome, and we took two men of her, the lifeboat went off in a tremendous gale from the north-east, but before we got there, three poor fellows had been drowned. We also took eleven men out of the lugger "Pet", which got on the Newcome in the early morning during the fishing season, the lugger being afterwards totally lost. There were also ten men rescued from an Italian brig (I have forgotten the name) which got on the bar of the Stanford. Beside these were several others- my memory fails me in telling the whole. We went away with two vessels, the crew of which we had saved, to Rochester and Harwich. We landed the crews of the Orwell and Amelia. I remember a smack getting on the Corton Sands, and we got twelve out of the fifteen men, the Corton boat taking three. Then there was the schooner Edina, laden with arsenic and coal. There were four life boats out that night after her. We got eight men out of her, and soon afterwards she went to pieces.

I now remember several others. In the year 1845 there was a small Danish schooner from which we took four hands. She was a total wreck, and sank on the Holm Sand. A French schooner on the Holm Sand went down; six hands taken off there in 1848. The Heart of Oak brig, on the Newcome Sands; Seven hands rescued there in 1848. There was a French brig on the Holm Sand also in 1857. We took off nine hands by the life boat. In 1859 a Colchester schooner, laden with iron was riding in distress, and we took off six of her crew. The brigantine Fly, of Shields, laden with fire clay, took off crew of seven in the same year. Then there was the Sea Pearl, a Danish vessel, laden with general cargo. Seven of the crew rescued in 1863. The brig Percy, of shields, coal laden. From this we took eight by the yawl in 1866, and another ten hands we rescued in the same year from a barque laden with oats from the Archangel. There was the Glenora, brig, of Scarborough, got on the Corton Patch in the afternoon of a day in November, 14 years ago. We boarded her with a small yawl, found we could do nothing with her, and asked them to leave. Captain said he would stop a little longer. They were compelled to go ashore, but before we got back the crew were urging us by flares. It was regular dirty night. We at last got to her, and took off eight men, and the next morning not a vestige of the vessel was to be seen.

In the December following, the barque Forest Flower, with Esparto grass, ran right into the stumps of the Glenora which were sticking out of the water. The life boat went out at once after her, and we succeeded in getting 17 off the wreck, the vessel becoming a total loss.

I must not forget the Berthon on the 14th November 1882, which struck on the Holm Sand soon after breakfast in a strong gale from the N.E. We saw her coming into danger, anticipated what would happen, and went off some time before she struck. She went into pieces within fifteen minutes after she had got on the sand; but we succeeded in getting off the crew of eight men. Thousands of people saw us at work, as it was broad daylight, and the Sand is right opposite the town. That was a narrow escape for the poor fellows, as hadn't we gone out when we did we couldn't have got there in time to be of any use.

That was about the last time I have been engaged. I am now 58 years old, and others have taken my place at present; but my heart is still in the work, and I am ready at any time to help when there's need, and nothing has given me more pleasure and satisfaction during my lifetime than trying to save life at sea. In 30 years my heart only stopped beating once, that was when we were approaching a wreck, making for the lee-side, a wave caught the lifeboat and carried it on to the vessels deck. At that point I thought the old boat might have broken its back, but no, the next wave caught the lifeboat and landed it safety on the lee-side, enabling us to rescue all the wrecked crew.

We have given the brave fellow's narrative as nearly as possible in his own words, those who know him will be able to verify; every statement, and as for his ability to render service, when we state he is 6ft.3in.high, and weighs 18 stone, it can easily be understood that when required to be put forth his herculean strength must have enabled him to render essential service in every respect.

Chapter Two

From birth to the later years

Robert's story begins with the birth of his father in the parish of Gunton in 1795, he was christened Robert Hook, and little is known of his younger years until at the age of 29 he married Miss Elizabeth Ellis on the 3rd May 1824. Their first child was named Betsey and was born in Gunton parish in August 1824, she married twice. Her first husband was John Nutter and second was Thomas Harrison who were married on the 5th January 1853 and she passed away in 1905 at the ripe age of 80.

Robert William Hook's., younger brother was born in December 1829 and was christen later that same month, William Ellis Hook, but throughout his life he was known by his nick-name Sheppey mainly because of the tan "slop" hat he wore. William married Amelia Wright when he was 21 years old in July 1850 and went on to have 13 children which 4 were boys. Both William and Amelia died a year after Robert William Hook in 1912.

Robert William Hook was born on the 4th June 1828 also in the parish of Gunton, he grew up in the beach village and lived with his parents in Denny's Score, now renamed Wildes Score. At the age of 5 robert was attending the school at the bottom of Wildes score, where he learned the basic skills of reading and writing, and by the age of sixteen Robert was 6 feet 3inches tall and he had a herculean frame and had already joined his father at the old company in saving lives. It was noted in the 1851 census that they had moved to 55 Whapload Way. In the 1853 England Census Robert was 23 years old and was still living with his parents, his sister Elizabeth and her husband John Nutter and my 4th great grand aunt's son Benjamin Butcher which was Robert's cousin, Robert senior and junior's occupation were both fisherman. In the same year Robert married Charlotte Boast and by 1861 Robert and his wife were living at the Rising-Sun where Robert's occupation on the 1861 census was down as a Fisherman and Beerhouse-keeper also Charlotte's sister, Harriet who was a shoe binder was lodging with them.

In the 1871 Census Robert was still Landlord of the Rising Sun but by the 1881 Census Robert had left the Rising Sun and moved opposite to the Fisherman's Arms but he was now a widower because on the 2nd October 1879 Charlotte passed away at the young age of 49. Back to 1881 Robert had taken over at the Fisherman's Arms but on March 17th, soon after his wife, Robert's father passes away at the age of 85. Later that year he married his housekeeper, Mrs Sarah Ann Goldsmith and adopted her 17-year-old son Charles and his sister Margaret, making them both Goldsmith-Hook.

In 1891, Robert was 63 and was still the landlord of the Fisherman's Arms, and at the time the 1891 census was taken, even though Robert put his lease up for sale in 1884, his change on mind in selling his lease was due to the fact of his reduced income from no longer being coxswain and the decline in sea traffic which the beach companies depended on for an income.

> Lot 5. Two COTTAGES, Nos. 43 and 44, Anguish-street, occupied by Edward Ceverly and Thomas Liffen, at weekly rents of 3s. 3d. = £17 15s. 4d. yearly.
> Lot 6. "The Fisherman's Arms," a well-known BEERHOUSE, situate on Whapload-road, in the occupation of Mr. Robert W. Hook, at the yearly rent of £30.
> Lot 7. A Piece of BUILDING LAND on Alexandra Estate, having a frontage of 40 feet next Regent-road, and a depth of 175 feet.

The Fisherman's Arms after Robert left carried on for a few more years but was soon to be converted into the Hammond's fish and chip shop, but in the 60's it was knocked down to make way for the Lowestoft cold store and today in 2015 it is an empty plot.

With the development of steam, more goods were travelling by rail, and steel hulled steam cargo ships had replaced the wooded brig. Skip forward ten years to the next census in 1901 and Robert had fully retired and at the age of 72 had moved to 125 St Peters Street, which is now in 2015 Humphries Hairdressers. This move to St Peters Street didn't last long and within a year or, so they had moved to No 32 Mariner's Street.

On the 2nd April 1911 census, just weeks before his death, Robert was 82 years old, Sarah Ann was 72, both had been married 30 years and Robert put his occupation as unable to work but by this time he was bed ridden.

Chapter Three

The press cuttings of a busy service.

LOWESTOFT REGATTA: - This annual, and now fashionable regatta, began on Tuesday 29th 1851, and attracted thousands of visitors to the town. An excursion train traversed the whole line of railway from London to Lowestoft, taking up passengers at every station. Several monster trains conveyed a vast number of people from Norwich, to the scene of amusement, and they soon spread themselves over the beach, the esplanade, and the new piers. The visitors had a delightful trip by a line of railway which presents, on each side, many objects of interest, many places associated with historical incidents, a great variety of rural scenery, and scenes of picturesque beauty. A good subscription of nearly £200 was raised for the prize fund, but a much larger amount is requisite in order to bring yachts of the first class to this part of the coast, and to leave a sufficient sum for the other matches and expenses. There was only one yacht entered," The Fanny," (Mr.Clay), and consequently there was no yacht match. First was the Yawl match, then the latteener match, then came the yacht and pleasure-boat match. After all those matches it was time for the punt match, this was for a purse of £10, to be contended for by sailing punts from all parts; the first punt to have £5; second, £3; and the third, £2. The following match started at 15.48 with the following punts: - Amity, Samuel Butcher, Lowestoft; Bruce, Charles Goodwin, Pakefield; Providence, Joseph Fletcher, Lowestoft; Providence, Thomas Butcher,

Lowestoft; Fawn, Robert Hook, Lowestoft; Finish, Samuel Mewse, Lowestoft; Gratitude, William Hook, Lowestoft; Emily, David Simpson, Southwold. The match created much amusement as many of the boats could make no way against the tide but were drifted in the wrong direction. The winning boats were- the Bruce, First; Amity, Second; Emily, Third. The final match was the rowing match, this was for a prize of £7, to be rowed for by six-oared beach gigs, from all parts. The first to have £4; second, £2; third, £1. Rather late in the afternoon the following started: - I'll Try, James Norman, Lowestoft; Beeswind, Daniel Durrant, Kessingland; Salem, Robert Hook, Lowestoft; Jenny Lind, John Mewse, Lowestoft.

John Mewse (Taken in 1893 wearing his Osip medal)

The crews rowed from stations opposite the pier southward to buoy and back again, a distance of two- and- a half miles.

The match was well contested and excited more interest than all proceeding. I'll try came in first by several lengths, Jenny Lind second, and beeswing third.

On Saturday 10th January 1852, the fine brig "Edward Kenny" of 254 tons, was totally wrecked on the Newcome Sands. The vessel which belonged to Wisbech, left Newcastle, for Venice, with coal on the 1st. On Saturday morning while off Kessingland, with the onset of bad weather, she bore up with other vessels in the Stamford channel, with the intention of taking Lowestoft roads as a place of safety. While running for the channel, the vessel suddenly struck the Sands. On seeing the vessel strike, the look-out at the Old Company shed raised the alarm, and several yawls put off to her assistance, with up to 50 hands they used every means possible to get her off, until low water without success; the vessel continued all the while to strike heavily. The wind increased to a gale, the sea made a complete breach over her, several of the yawls which already had many of the Lifeboat crew on board then returned for the Lowestoft Lifeboat, but before this could be done the position of the brig's crew became so immediately perilous, that they were obliged to jump into a large yawl, still lying by them, and succeeded with great risk in reaching Pakefield, through heavy surf, and with a boat half full of water. The only thing saved from her was the rigging and the name board, which was then screwed to the Old Company shed.

On Saturday 31st January 1852, the galliot "Ioni", Capt slos the master, of and from Hookseil, for London, assisted in leaky by the Old Company beachmen, the latter claimed salvage, the former says his flag was up for a gat pilot only.

A melancholy catastrophe occurred off Lowestoft at about noon on Thursday 7th October 1852. The schooner "Harriet and Jane," Shee, of Youghal, from Aberdeen, for London, with stone, had been on the ridge and was assisted off by the beach-men of the old company, and while proceeding to the harbour, she foundered. About twenty persons were on board, and was reported at the time four were drowned, one of the brig's crew, and two beach-men named Henry Butcher and William Cook, and Mr.Reeve, clerk to the firm of Messrs, Small and Fry. The main boom of the schooner caught the stern of the yawl, and, had it not divided so as to flap down, she must have gone down with her, and several of the beach-men were injured.

On Friday 12th November 1852, it was blowing hard with terrible driving rain along the Lowestoft coast. At about 4 p.m., one of those heart-rending catastrophes unfolded, a wreck with the loss of all hands in full sight of shore, took place off Lowestoft. The unfortunate vessel was the brig "Wear Packet", Cames, of and from Sunderland, for London with coals, having on board a crew of seven hands. It was supposed that the brig scrapped her bottom on parts of a sunken wreck, in passing through the Stanford Channel at low water, and afterwards making water so rapidly the crew to prevent her going down in deep water, they ran her onto the Newcome Sand. Long before this, a signal of distress was put up, and two yawls from two beach companies immediately went off, but due to the bad temper of the sea this day, they both could not get near them by at least a quarter of a mile; they therefore obliged to return without being able to render any assistance. Before they reached the shore, Lieutenant. Joachim offered to go with any crew that would man the Lifeboat. This call fell on deaf ears and didn't meet with a response, as the case was then looked upon as hopeless: In addition to which the coxswain and all the best of the men were out in their own company yawls attempting a rescue. After the yawls returned and reached shore, another effort was made to induce a crew to go off in the Lifeboat. Mr.G.S.Gowing volunteered to accompany them and give them £5. Another gentleman offered them £1 a man. Mr. James Peto would give them £5 for every man of crew saved. Every inducement that was generously offered was unavailing. Robert said, "was there a chance of saving them," "We would go." There would have been no problem or difficulty in obtaining a crew had it appeared to the brave Lifeboat men that there was a possibility of their exertions being rewarded by the saving of the poor fellows from a watery grave. While this conversation with the coxswain and beach-men was going on at 6 p.m., part of the upper decks of the ill-fated brig had washed ashore at Kessingland, and at 8 p.m., heavy timbers, picked up on that beach, denoted how rapidly the work of destruction had gone on, and left but faint hopes as to the safety of the crew. The harbour steam-tug was out ready to have taken the Lifeboat in tow had she been launched.

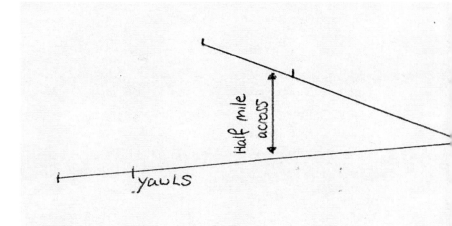

In the above diagram, showing the relative position of the vessel and the yawls. - E.N.N. The first mark on the top line denotes where the brig touched the ridge, and the second where she run aground. The bottom line shows where the yawls started and were they got to, were the lines intersect is the point where they hoped to meet; between the two lines is sand and broken water, in which no yawl could live.

On Saturday 18th December 1852, the brig "Miriam," John Mugford master, of Sunderland from Hartlepool for Southampton, when riding in Yarmouth roads, drove her stern into the bows of a laden brig, tearing away her stern frame, stanchion, bulwark, and rail, notwithstanding she continued her voyage after she cleared; she reached the knock, and was obliged to put back, making water, and while passing through the Lowestoft roads on Sunday, she struck on the inner shoal, and after raising her distress was assisted off by beach-men of the Old Company.

Shipwreck, On Saturday 5th January 1853, the schooner "Mary," master. Mr. Pearce, of and for Ipswich from Sunderland, when taking the Stanford channel, she grounded on the Holm-head, beating heavily she unshipped her rudder. She afterwards beat over the sand, but in consequence of being unmanageable, she drove onto the Newcome, where she became a total wreck. The harbour tug towed out the Lowestoft Lifeboat through heavy sea and gale force wind. Her crew of six men and a boy were saved by the Lowestoft and pakefield Lifeboat's which arrived at the same time. Mr. D. H. Fry. Esq., presented the crew of each lifeboat £5. This was the first time the Victoria, the new Lowestoft Lifeboat had been used. Her crew stated that she was deficient in weight on her keel, and her masts and sails not suitable, being those of the old one, which was a much smaller boat. Coxswain Robert Hook stated, "if a sea should catch the sails, the mast would break like a carrot."

On Monday 25th April 1853, Lowestoft was visited with such a heavy gale of wind from the E.N.E. and N.E., accompanied with pitiless storms of rain as we have scarcely had during winter. Several trees were up-rooted by its fury, and the following, among other casualties, occurred to shipping. Several vessels parted with their anchors in our roads, and proceeded South-wards. The brig "Mary Young," Thomas Knox, Master, 285tons burthen, of and from Sheild's for Genoa, arrived in Yarmouth roads on Sunday, and proceeded to Stanford Channel on Monday, but was compelled to anchor from the Violence of the gale, on doing so the chain parted, and before the next could take hold, she drifted near the Newcome Sand, when a 3rd anchor let go, which brought her up, at low water she struck upon the sand, and unshipped her rudder. A signal was made for assistance, when Robert Hook and his fellow beach-men manned the lifeboat, and proceeded to her, and with some difficulty reached her. The crew at first refused to leave her, but subsequently they did so, and were landed about 8.30pm. Attempts were made next morning to get her off, but without success. At night, having thrown a considerable quantity of her cargo of coal overboard, she came off, and was, by the assistance of the beach-men and the harbour company's two steam tugs, brought her into the harbour, and about eleven o'clock on Wednesday morning was removed into the inner basin.

On Thursday 28th July 1853, the brig "Vivid," John Smith Norris, of Dover, from Newcastle for Portsmouth, whilst beating to windward, missed stays and took the ground on Corton Sand. She was afterwards assisted off, their own efforts being unavailable, by the united Old and Young Companies of beach-men, and brought up in the roads making no water. Being a smart vessel, it took considerable trouble in getting her off, the men asked for £400 for their services. The sum of £150 was offered and not accepted, and it was settled by the Admiralty court.

On Monday 13th February 1854, the brig "Kathleen", of and from Hartlepool, for London, was assisted off the Holm-Sand

and into the harbour, by the Old Company of beach-men.

On the morning of Wednesday 15th February 1854, the brig "Fly," which was stranded on Lowestoft beach during the heavy snow storm of the 4th, was got off by the Old Company. It would be another 7 years and she would meet her end at Lowestoft.

At about twelve o'clock on Sunday morning of the 11th March 1855, the "Octavia," a schooner, belonging to the Yarmouth harbour- master, got on the Holm-Sand. She was assisted off by the Old Company of beach-men, without sustaining damage either to her timbers or her cargo, which consisted of barley.

The annual marine regatta, which has been growing in popularity and it has now become one of the best on the Eastern Coast, came off on Tuesday 24th July 1855. "A cloudy sky and a Southerly wind", though particularly favourable on a hunting morning, are scarcely to be desired on a regatta day, and when, as on a Tuesday, there was the unwanted addition of a down pour of drizzle. The effect of the inclement weather was evident in the decreased number of excursionist visitor's; but still the trains came, and the early trains where full to overflowing. The number of visitors from Norwich were somewhere in the number of 1500 and would have been a lot more if the weather had been fine. Never-the-less the esplanade, pier, and the beach beyond, and in fact every point from were an uninterrupted view of the sea could be obtained, were lined with onlookers; and the towns

Hotels, Inns and boarding houses appeared to be full to overflowing with visitors. The first match was for a prize of a plate, value 100 Guineas, to be sailed for by schooner yachts belonging to the Royal yacht club. Coming in as follows; Georgiana, Portsmouth; Mayfly, London; Coquette, Liverpool. The second match was for a prize plate, valued at 30 sovereigns, for yachts, not exceeding 50 tons. They finished as follows; Thought, Avalon and Maude; all the yachts were from London. A purse of 30 sovereigns was offered for yawls, but at the hour for starting, but only two, the Princess Victoria, of Yarmouth, and the Eclipse, of Lowestoft had entered, and as the regulations required that four should start, so there was no race at that point. The Queen Victoria, of Yarmouth; Royal Standard and the Cambridge Lass also from Yarmouth, came up sometime afterwards. There was what appeared to be a great deal of jealousy and ill feeling amongst the members of the different companies of beach-men, as well as between those of rival ports. At some point one lot of beach-men called the other beach-men "a bunch of pirates", and punches were thrown, which lead to the above match being cancelled, and spoiled what is generally the prettiest match of the day. After a few further matches the final match was between beach gigs. This was the most exciting race for the long-shore spectators, but, like the yawl match, had nearly been spoiled by the ill feeling amongst the beach-men. A purse of 20 sovereigns was offered, to be rowed for in heats, the first boat to receive £12, the second £5, and the 3rd £3. Both heats were won easily by the "Teaser", of Southwold, Robert and the Old Company came second in the," I'll Try", and the "Kate", of Lowestoft 3rd, a result which was mainly gained by the Teaser being double banked, or two men to each oar, while the others had but one. On the second day Wednesday, a grand review of the yachts took place in the roads, and a rowing match for beach gigs was got up. The number of company's present was very much less than that of the previous day, but still the excursion trains brought several hundreds, and both piers were well covered with spectators. There was a cool breeze, and the review of yachts, was commenced at one o'clock, was a very pretty sight, each boat displaying to its best, its sailing qualities. The match for beach gigs was competed for by the "Jenny lind", "I'll try", "Welcome Home", "Quebec", and the "Prince". Both heats were won easily by Robert in the "Jenny Lind", and not surprising as it was manned by Lifeboat crew. At the after-dinner speeches, Captain. Steward congratulated the committee on the result of the regatta, which he thought had been quite as successful as regattas generally were: but there was one exception, the yawl race; and he regretted it, for it was a race which always excited great interest and pleasure. He was only sorry that the failure had been on this occasion been some misunderstanding between the Lowestoft and Yarmouth men. The Lowestoft men had, he thought, been unusually sensitive in their notions of pride, and he wished heartily they would get rid of them, or only exercise them on those occasions when the saving of human life was involved.

Lowestoft Humane Society. The anniversary of the Suffolk Humane Society and Lowestoft Lifeboat Association was held on Monday 14th Sept 1855, when the Lowestoft and Pakefield lifeboats where afloat for the Society to inspect. The annual meeting was held at the Crown Hotel in Lowestoft High Street, Sir Edward. Gooch, was presiding. It was agreed that the lifeboat should be kept afloat in the harbour during the winter months, suitably protected by a canvas cover.

The following awards were made for lives saved: William. Cook along with his son and grandson, received 2s.6d each, for rescuing a young lady from the water, as she slipped off the stairs into the harbour, the grandson also received another 2s.6d for saving a young boy who fell off a raft.

Mr. Daniel. West, a bridge-man jumped into the lock after Mrs. Munds who had mistook the lights, but for his effort, she would have been drowned.

An award was for Robert. William. Hook and Robert. Wright received 10 shillings for saving Samuel Butcher, whose punt was upset entering the harbour, as reported at the time. The harbour pilots, Porter, Golder, Swan and Butcher, also received 10 shillings for saving William. Ayres, who was also in the above punt when she turned over.

Robert was also awarded 2s.6d for saving Daniel Mitchells from the harbour in April 1854. All members and their friends dined at the Crown Hotel at the end of the meeting.

On Saturday 24th November 1855 the Norfolk Chronicle reported on the adjudication of the brig "Planet." A somewhat interesting case of salvage came before Charles Steward and Robert Cook Fowler, Esq., at our court room's, on Tuesday, for adjudication. On the 3rd November the brig "Planet," Thos.Holmes, master from Sunderland, from Memel for London, with tallow and copper, as having been assisted into Lowestoft with loss of anchors, and that these having been supplied, she proceeded on her voyage, and while going out of the Stanford channel the wind died off, causing her to take the ground on the Newcome Sands, where, in the course of the night, she became a perfect wreck, and that a large quantity of her tallow was, on the following morning, picked up on Corton beach. The case which was reported had arisen out of the salving of that part of her cargo which consisted of copper.

Mr.W.R.Seago, appeared on behalf of the salvors - Robert Hook and Benjamin Neave, and others; Captain. Small and Lloyd's agent, appeared on behalf of the owners of the "Planet," and others concerned. Before going into the case, Mr.Small remarked that, so far from the salvors being entitled to remuneration for the property salved, they were open to prosecution for interfering with it at all, in as much as the "Planet" and her cargo were under the charge and protection of the receiver of Admiralty droits. Mr.Seago, in reply, called the attention of the bench to the 144th Clause of the Merchant Shipping Act, which states that, "whenever any ship is stranded or in distress in any place on the shore of the sea, the receiver should, forthwith, proceed to such place, and see." Mr.Small contended that the "Planet" was not stranded on shore of the sea, and was, to all intents and purposes, a derelict, both the vessel and that portion of cargo being under water upon the Newcome Sands, and abandoned by the crew. The bench having taken Mr.Seago's view of the matter, and the value of the copper salved being agreed between the parties as at £201, being at the rate of one shilling per pound for the quantity salved (over 35 cwt.), the percentage for salvage upon that amount was then argued. Mr.Small suggested that 20 percent, was all that ought to be awarded, in the case of an arrangement having been made by him Mr.Wilton, for salving the copper at that rate. Mr.Seago on behalf of his clients, alluded to the law generally acted upon in cases of derelict property, under which, a moiety of the value was awarded to the salvors, and cited several cases in proof. He called attention to a case at Yarmouth, some two years since, in which the cargo was tallow, and where an award of a fourth was made for that picked up in the harbour, a third for that found on the beach, and a half for that recovered at sea. He reminded the bench, that in the case of the tallow belonging to this vessel, the "Planet," £8 per cask had been given for chalking those casks, which had been picked up at Corton beach; he had no doubt men might have been found who would have done it for a less sum; but if they had been so paid, where the labour was nominal, was it to be argued that these men, who, at great risk and labour, had dredged this copper up from the hold of the vessel, were to receive only 20 percent, because another party had agreed to do it for that sum, but which he had failed in doing.

He also remarked to the bench that Hook and these men had, without reward, saved the crew of the "Planet" by the use of the lifeboat, and that in launching their yawl to render her assistance one poor man lost his life. (It was stated at the time that, owing to a sea catching the yawl, she fell upon two of the men, and that one, named Cook, was so seriously injured as not to be expected to live; Cook died a day or two afterwards.)

He therefore hoped that under these circumstances an award of a moiety would be made to his clients. The magistrates having consulted a short time, awarded a net third, which amounted to £67.5 shillings, and costs £5.15 shillings. 6d.

On Wednesday 21st May 1856 the Bury and Norwich post reported on the adjudication before C.Steward and F.Leathes, Esq at our Court rooms. The first was that the brig "Regina," Captain Pratt, of Sunderland. Mr Seago opened the case by stating that the salvors, William Gallant, Robert Hook, and their company, were at their boat shed on Lowestoft beach, about eight o'clock on the evening of May the 7th, when they observed the brig Regina coming round the ness under fore-topsail, and foretop mast stay sail with loss of an anchor; the wind blowing a heavy gale with rain from the E.N.E, and a heavy sea, and fancying that she would make for Lowestoft harbour, and finding it impossible to launch a boat, the salvor at once ran down to the harbour as fast as they could, as they believed the vessel could not get in without doing damage. As soon as the brig entered the harbour, the anchor was let go with about twenty fathoms of chain, which from the violence of the sea and rolling swell would not hold her, and she commenced driving so fast to leeward, the salvors immediately manned a boat and boarded her. They offered their services to the captain, and he said, "I will give you £10," which the salvors refused to accept, and offered to leave it to the gentlemen on shore. At this time, the vessel was striking fore and aft, and beating heavily against the pier doing the pier and herself considerable injury. Mr. Balls, the deputy harbour master then came up, and complained to the captain of the injury done, and asked him why he did not employ salvors, and whether he knew what damage he was doing to the pier, when the captain made answer and said," I have offered them £10 which they refused," and Mr. Balls replied "Well I shall hold you responsible for all damage you're now doing to the pier as you have assistance and will not employ them." The captain then said, "Well run away a warp and get her off as fast as you can." Salvors were on hand to run away a warp to windward, to haul away a large hawser (a thick rope or cable for mooring or towing a ship) which was at once made fast, and as many hands were put to the windlass (winch) as could stand there, and it required several hands to hold on the hawser to make it nip, whilst the others were heaving.

Salvors then took the warp to a double purchase winch, and

commenced heaving at that with a number of hands holding on and heaving; during the time the captain was urging salvors to greater exertion, heaving upon the warp and hawser, as he was fearful from the vessel striking so heavily that she would knock her rudder off and he was assured that the men were doing all that could be done. After a short time, the vessel was got clear of the ground and moved. The vessel having dragged her anchor so to leeward salvors were obliged to slip from it, and upon getting the vessel over to windward they moored her with two parts of the hawser and two parts of the warp, as it still continued to blow with great fury.

On the following morning, salvors got the anchor, weighing upwards of 11 cwt, with 11 fathoms of chain cable, and put them on board the brig. During the time these services were being performed, there were 67 of the old company engaged. He also stated that there was an unusually high tide, and that had the vessel not then been got off she would have still remained. Captain Rouse put in an affidavit of the captain and his wife and two of the crew, under the 9th clause of the merchant marine Act, and contended that there had been a specific agreement entered into by the captain, for their services for £20. - Mr. Seago denied that any agreement had been entered into; -The court awarded £45, each party paying their own costs.

The next case was that of the schooner "Samson" of Cowes, Thomas Brown, Master, for services rendered by Norman, Hook and their company, on Thursday May 8th. It appeared that the schooner, having lost her foremast, topmast, while off Flamborough Head, and being in considerable danger of running ashore, was taken in tow by the steam-tug, and conducted into the Lowestoft roads. When the vessel got near the Stanford Light-Ship, and in the stream of the Newcombe-Sand, the steam tug let go, the schooner having aft sails on her.

 The Captain endeavoured to weather the neck of the Newcombe Sand, but fearing, from the flood tide being so strong, he could not do it, let go his anchor and hoisted a signal just below the eve of the main rigging, which the salvors saw, and at once launched their gig which was nearly capsized from the heavy sea rolling in, caused by the gale of the proceeding day. After the salvors got alongside the schooner, there was an arrangement made for them to fetch a steam tug to tow the vessel into the harbour. The salvors left four of their company on board the vessel and proceeded to the harbour, and made an agreement with the steam-tug to conduct the vessel into the harbour for £6. Hook along with 9 other company members went on the steam-tug to assist, the steam-tug returned with the schooner by half past twelve o'clock the same day into Lowestoft harbour, and safely moored. Captain Small in defence contested that there had been no agreement between the parties, that the vessel was not in a dangerous position, and that the captain hoisted the signal for a steam-tug and not for Hook and his beach company.

On cross examination of the captain of the schooner it

appeared that he had engaged the salvors, and had made a minute on a piece of paper as to what the agreement was. The court awarded the salvors £15, out of which they must pay the steam-tug £6, each party to pay their own costs.

The Late Gales. -Lowestoft had strong winds from the North and North-West, accompanied with snow squalls, heavy seas, and on Tuesday 25th November 1856 Lowestoft had the highest tide it had ever experienced for a long time. These were preceded on Sunday evening by one of the most gorgeous and magnificent sunset's that locals remember to have witnessed, and which was considered the fore-runner of a heavy gale. The high tide Tuesday washed away considerable portions of the Corton cliffs, endangering some of the outbuildings on Mr.Wood's farm. At Gunton the sea broke over onto the Denes, which were soon inundated, and flowing on, covering the Denes and Cricket-ground, and passed on beyond Mr.Gowing's tar-house, the water being deep enough to allow a punt to be rowed upon it. The water flowed so rapidly as to cover a number of nets laid out to dry, and the fisherman might be seen hauling them, but minus fish. At the harbour it covered the inner pier, and washed away all the empty herring barrels from the vicinity of the fish market. Considerable damage was done to the coping of the bastion and inclined walk down to the beach opposite the Royal Hotel. The beach had been excavated to a depth of four or five feet below the foot of the above inclined walk, rendering a ladder necessary to reach the beach without dropping or jumping down. Titan at present stood unmoved on his solid pedestal, but another such attack by Old Ocean might prostrate him. The broad concrete walk at the foot of the cliffs leading to Pakefield had been much damaged, the sea having undermined it, causing large blocks of it to sink. While the Lifeboat is afloat within its boat-shed the gallant crew and coxswain Robert Hook helped out the beach community.

 The brig "Tenant", of Stockton, from Dantzie for London with timber, got upon the North part of the Newcome- Sand about noon on Monday 5th January 1857. A yawl went to her assistance, but they services were declined. About 3 p.m. a signal of distress was hoisted, when the Lifeboat was launched and proceeded to her, and having anchored to windward of her, dropped down under her stern and succeeded in taking out half her crew, when in a tremendous squall the cable parted; but the Lifeboat having taken a strong rope from the brig as a guide, she was enabled to hold till the rest of the crew were taken in, with the exception of the master, who, in attempting to get into the Lifeboat was washed overboard, and was with considerable difficulty rescued and hauled into the boat in a senseless state, after having more than once disappeared under the waves. Sail was then made for the harbour for the more expeditiously landing the master, who had scarcely shown any signs of life. He was taken to the Harbour Inn, and through the unwearied exertions of W.C. Worthington, Esq., and his assistant, suspended animation was replaced with strong signs of life. The conduct of the crew of the Lifeboat was admirable. The following day the brig "Darlington," Chicken, master, of and from shields for London, came ashore about 7 a.m. of Tuesday, opposite the High-Light; The Lifeboat launched but the crew were saved by the coastguard before it arrived.

On Saturday 17th January 1857 in the Norfolk Chronicle there was a report on the adjudication on Wednesday 14th, the following cases were brought before Charles Steward & R.C. Fowler, Esq., at our court house;- The first heard was that of the brig "Naples Packet," of Maldon, from Hartlepool for London, with coals, James Harrison, master. John Clowes, Esq., of Yarmouth, appeared for the salvors, William Gallant and Robert Hook, of this place, and their company of beach-men; Wm. Seago, Esq., for the vessel. The value agreed upon was- Vessel £800, and cargo £150. The sum claimed by the salvors was £180. Mr.Clowes read a statement on behalf of his clients, which, with the exception of one main point, that the brig had a spare anchor weighing 9 cwt, ready at her bows to let go, differed but little from that made from that made on the part of the vessel. Mr. Clowes observed that he rested his claim on the amount of property saved-nearly £1000, on the lives of the crew saved, and also upon the risk the beach-men ran of their own lives and property in the services rendered; and also upon the skill that had been shown by his clients in rendering services. It was true the time they were engaged was not long, but through their skill the vessel was brought into the harbour. The bench said, that asking the enormous sum of £180 for salvage was a folly. They awarded them £45, and expenses £5.15s, making

£50.15s., for the vessel to pay.

Second case was the brig "Tenant". -This vessel drove upon the Newcome Sand during the late gale, was assisted off on Saturday morning by Hook and the old beach company, and thence into the inner harbour about 11am, by two steam tugs, the Tenant had lost her rudder & was water logged. The cargo, Timber was rafted ashore later that day. They Were happy to state that Captain Laine, master of the above vessel, who was hauled into the Lowestoft Lifeboat in a senseless state by Hook in his other role as coxswain, had partly recovered.

It was reported in the Norfolk chronicle, Saturday January 18th, 1857. About noon on Thursday, as the brig "Lonisa" of Lynn, from Sunderland for London, was passing through the Stanford Channel she missed the stays, and from lightness of wind and strength of tide, took the ground on the holm Sand. Being unable to get the vessel off, the old company lead by Hook, were employed, who, after using the accustomed appliance, succeeded in floating her, and received £50 for their service.

At the Admiralty Court, Thursday May 21st, 1857 a case was promoted by the Old Company of Lowestoft against the schooner "Dahlia" to procure salvage remuneration for services rendered to her on the 5th December 1856 on the Newcome-Sand. The schooner, laden with pig lead, was bound from Seville to Newcastle. The salvors, as they represented, finding it impossible to conduct the vessel into

Lowestoft harbour, ran her ashore near the lower lighthouse, and then entered into an agreement to land the stores and cargo and securely warehouse them, and get the lighten schooner into harbour for £300. It was afterwards found necessary to lay a false deck in order to refloat the schooner, and the agent for the owners inquired of the salvors what they would pay towards the expenses, but they declined to have anything to do with it. The agent then entered into contract with a local shipwright for the false deck, and the schooner, having been got off the beach, was towed by a steam-tug into the harbour. On the part of the owners, it was contended that the salvors had, in the first instance, forced themselves on board the schooner and taken possession of her against the remonstrances of the master, but, there being no other assistance which could be procured, the agreement in question was subsequently entered into. The salvors and their spokesman Robert Hook who was also the coxswain of the Lifeboat in reply, averred that they were hailed to board the schooner, and were assisted in doing so by ropes thrown in their boat. The owner made a tender of £202, deducting from the agreement £98, the expense of the false deck. The value of the property salved was £1.250. Dr. Robinson and Dr. Jenner were heard for the salvers; Dr. Adams and Dr. Twiss for the owners. The learned Judge was of opinion that the salvors were bound to pay for the false deck, it being one of the appliances necessary in order to get the schooner into the harbour, and, had the case rested there, he would have pronounced, anterior services, for which he would award £100, with costs.

The Norfolk Chronicle on Saturday 18th July 1857 reported on an adjudication on Wednesday, the case of the schooner "Sarah," John Thompson, master from Seaham, of and for Poole, was adjudicated before R.C.Fowler and James. Peto. Esq., The salvors, William Gallant, Robert Hook, and their company, were represented by W.R.Seago, Esq.; C.H Chamberlin, Esq., of Great Yarmouth representing the owners of the vessel. It appeared that the above vessel ran upon the Corton Sand to the south of the north-west home chequered buoy, about 1.30pm., on Sunday. The salvors went off to her, and the master of the vessel finding his own efforts to get off ineffectual, subsequently engaged their assistance, the remuneration for their services being agreed to be referred to the authorities on shore. The salvors went to work in their usual way of laying anchors, without success. It became necessary to lighten her, by throwing overboard a portion of her coals, after which she came off about noon on the following day (Monday), and was brought to anchor in our south roads. The salvors accompanied by the master of the vessel, went over to Yarmouth to endeavor to affect an arrangement with agent-Messrs, Butcher and son- but without success. It was admitted by the salvors that the crew of the Sarah had assisted in getting the vessel off. The matter having been heard on both sides, the court awarded the salvors £110, and costs £5.15s.

On the week commencing 28th December 1857, the schooner "George", J. Kerson, master, of and for Southampton from Shields, with coals, while proceeding through the Stanford channel, came to ground on the Holm-Sand. The Old Company immediately proceeded to her assistance, and after the usual appliances were brought into operation, they succeeded in getting her off, after which she was conducted into port by the harbour tug. Her compasses, from some cause, were found three points out of calibration. The following day as the schooner "Ann and Mary", Samuel Jones, master, of Chester, from Goole for Gosport, with flagstones, was sailing through the inner channel of the South-road's, intending to pass out at Pakefield Gat, she approached too near the edge of the Newcome-Sand, and it being dead low water and very smooth, she grounded. Robert and the Old Company along with the harbour tug conducted her into port.

The brig "Oswy" was wrecked on Corton Sand's, near Lowestoft, during a gale of wind on Thursday 25th February 1858. The Lowestoft Lifeboat under Robert Hook was towed out by a steam-tug, and the brig was found in a perilous situation under the beach, flat, and only one anchor left. The Lifeboat took out her crew, consisting of six hands. The brig came onto the beach at Gunton during the evening, and became a total wreck.

On Wednesday, March 3rd, 1858, the above simple rescue ended-up in the Lowestoft Police Court, and was as follows: Before Chas. Steward (Chairman), Edward. Leathes, and J. Peto. Esqs. Captain Thomas Small; Lloyds agent at this port, appeared before the bench, observing that he did at under rather disagreeable circumstances which took place on

Corton beach, on Thursday night, of the 25th, at the wreck of the brig "Oswy", of Shoreham, Parkhurst master. It appeared that the "Oswy" was riding off Corton by one anchor, having lost her other. A signal was made for assistance, when a yawl was launched, and subsequently the Lifeboat, which was manned by the beach-men of the united Old and Young companies, and towed by the harbour tug to the Holm-Sand, and from there to the brig, which had drifted in near shore, the wind blowing a heavy gale from the East. The master and crew were taken into the Lifeboat, and towed back into harbour by the steam tug. Shortly after the crew had been landed, the vessel parted from her remaining anchor, and came ashore a little to the North of Gunton Warren-house. Captain Small went on to state, that upon her coming to the beach, an immense number of men, something like 200, collected, and seeing so many, he dispatched a person for the Chief officer of the Coast-guard at Corton, and another for the receiver of Admiralty Droits. The Captain and him-self requested the Chief-Officer (Fenton Hake, Esq.), to allow his men to guard the property from interference. He Mr. Small remained there a considerable time, and as the water was receding, it became necessary to make arrangements for having the vessel stripped in order to ease her; and as he thought it only just that the persons who had rescued the lives, should have the preference in salving the property, he sent for the Lowestoft coxswain, "Hook", and made arrangements with him and his company (Old Company). Shortly after this the North-Road company of beach-men went to Corton, brought down a boat, and insisted upon launching it. He (Mr. Small) had to call upon the officers to use all their force to prevent it, and even to exhibit their fire arms. Unfortunately, these beach-men ran away with the idea, that every vessel coming ashore or getting on the sands, though being left by the crew only with a view of saving their lives, and with the intention of returning again to her, was a derelict, and the property of any beach-man that got on board her. It was impossible for him to describe to the Bench the state of disorder that was on the beach, but they could imagine that when he said there were 100 men pulling the boat one way, and 100 pulling her the other, and at last the coast-guard were compelled to draw their pistols and cutlasses for protection. He (Mr. Small) remonstrated with the beach-men, and begged of them not to act so. He also had to send and bring the receiver to try and quell the disturbance. He (Mr. Small) must say, that nothing could exceed the cool courage and great forbearance of the Chief-officer of the Coast-guard and his men. One of the beach-men was nearly drowned, and three others were much injured. He wished the bench to caution the ringleaders in this affair, he did not wish to prosecute, but he was not certain that ulterior proceedings would not be taken by the board of trade. He was fully empowered to take steps he had, by the 441st, 444th, and 445th sections of the wreck and salvage Act. He really felt that something dreadful was going to occur. Had any of the men been shot it would have been entirely their own affair. Thomas Rose., William Rose., and Daniel Knight, of the North-Road Company, were addressed as follows, by the chairman: I think both the receiver and Capt. Small have acted with great forbearance in coming here to make these statements, so that we might offer you a few words of advice. It is quite necessary that you and your beach-men should understand that you have no business whatever to touch any ship that is stranded, so long as the receiver, or coast-guard, or agent, or owner is present to give direction. And. moreover, all of you are bound to attend to the instruction which may be given you by the receiver as to the protection of the property. You have no right to lay a hand upon it, and if you do persevere in touching that property, they have a right to prevent your doing so by the strongest measures possible. They have the right to cut you down- a right to shoot you, in the same way you would shoot a man who was breaking into your house. With respect to Mr. Hake, the chief Coast-guard officer, who appears to be present, I think he acted with most extraordinary forbearance.

Adjudication. On Monday the claims of Robert Hook, Richard Butcher, Matthew Colman, and others, Lowestoft beach-men, for services rendered on the 8th March 1858., to the brig "Friendship," of Shield's, -Wright, master, were adjudicated before R.C. Fowler, and Edward Leathes, Esq., at the court-house. Mr. Seago appeared for the salvors, and Mr. Chamberlin, of Yarmouth, for the owners of the vessel, which was 267 tons registered, and the value of which was, after some discussion, agreed at £500. Mr. Seago, however, observed that if she was not worth £3 per ton, she was unfit for sea. From the statement put in by Mr. Seago, and from which Mr. Chamberlin did not materially dissent, it appeared that between two and three a.m., of Monday the 8th, during the severe hurricane, Robert Hook observed three pitched heads burning from three vessels, as he supposed, on the Newcome-Sand, the Stanford Light vessel at the same time throwing out blue Lights, and a steam-boat at anchor in the roads throwing up rockets. As no other boats could at the time float with safety, Hook and the salvors launched the lifeboat, and proceeded through the fearful surf on the beach towards the endangered vessel, with a four-reefed foresail and mizzen only. On approaching the sand, they observed a schooner sunk there, with her mast playing so as to dip her top sail in the water. Not being able to ascertain if any were in the rigging they laid by her till day-light, when perceiving none of them there, they proceeded to the "Friendship," one of the vessel's that had been burning a light, but was not when the salvors boarded her. It appeared that the brig had blown partly over the sand, had beaten heavily upon it, and was making water, and had lost one anchor. On board of this vessel where the crew of the schooner "Orwell", by which the lifeboat had been lying. The lifeboat took the crew into it, and landed them in Lowestoft harbour, seven of the crew of the lifeboat being left on board to assist the brig into the harbour, and on its arrival, then others also of their company assisted in getting out warps etc. Mr.Seago, on behalf of his clients, urged that very valuable services had been rendered, and that the time of those services had been rendered, and that the time of those services commenced with the launching of the lifeboat. Mr. Chamberlin on the other hand, while admitting that services had been rendered, which ought to receive due reward, never the less contended that the services commenced from the time of boarding, and that his clients ought not be expected to pay for the launching of the boat for saving the lives of a crew, whom his clients had received on board their vessel, and who, if they had not ungratefully refused to assist in getting the brig into harbour, might have prevented the necessity of employing the salvors at all. This was flatly contradicted by the master of the "Orwell," who stated that his-self and crew where perfectly willing to have assisted, and offered to do so, but their services were not accepted. The court awarded the sum of £70 and costs £6. The chairman (R.C.Fowler, Esq.) remarked that the conduct of the salvors was very meritorious in going off in such a gale of wind. He should not have liked to have been in the boat. Although they had made that award, they were not quite sure that they were justified in doing so, as the lifeboat was now connected with the National Lifeboat Society.

On the 13th March 1858, the schooner "Gipsey", William. Shenton, of Exeter, in ballast for Sunderland, got upon the Newcome-Sand, in consequence of having to pass under a barque's stern; assisted off by the Old Company for £60.

At a meeting of the Royal National Lifeboat Institution, on the 1st April 1858., the following rewards were granted for saving life.-A reward of £19.5s was voted to the crew of the Lowestoft Lifeboat, for their praiseworthy conduct in rescuing during a hurricane the crew of five men of the sloop

"Orwell," of Arbroath, which was wrecked on the Newcome Sands on the 17th March; immediately on the return of the Lifeboat to the shore with the shipwrecked crew, she again put off with her gallant crew to the assistance of another vessel which was seen on the sands, but which had fortunately been driven over, and therefore did not require the help of the Lifeboat. A reward of £14 was likewise granted to the crew of the same lifeboat for rescuing 12 men from the brig "Oswy" of Shoreham, which during a heavy gale of wind, was wrecked off Corton Sands.

On Tuesday 18th May 1858, at about 9 p.m., the wind was blowing strong from the West and by North, the brigantine "one," of Sunderland, in reaching through the Stanford Channel, grounded on the Holm Head. She was observed by the Old Company of beach-men, who proceeded to her assistance, and under an agreement for £220, succeeded in getting her off and anchoring her in the North Roads, at between one and two a.m., on Wednesday. Robert did comment when asked by a reporter from the paper. "We have had been a long time without a job, but at last we have had one."

The brigantine "Agnus," of 82tons register, Captain Bervie, of Wigton, From Shields for Galway, with a cargo of coals, bricks, and clay, owing to the heavy rain he mistook the red buoy of the Newcome Sands for the chequered buoy of the Holm Sand and came aground about 2 p.m., of Friday 20th August 1858; assistance was quickly offered by Lowestoft pilots and beach-men of the Old Company, but the wind and sea freshening, she forged further on the sand and sank about an hour afterwards. Robert and the Old Company manage to save part of the cargo and the crew; the next day Saturday, they were forwarded to their homes by Wm.Cole. Esq., the honorary agent of the Shipwrecked Mariners Society. The next day Saturday, the galliot "Undaunted," Captain Gasttom, from London for Hartlepool, in ballast, owing to the strong wind from the South-East she was driven ashore at the Ness-Point right in front of the Old Company shed. The beach-men of that company went to her assistance, and after the usual appliances had been brought into the harbour at about midnight. Just as they removed the "Undaunted," a French schooner "Marie Mathilda," Captain Dojon, of Nantes, from Dunkirk for Sunderland, in ballast, also drove on shore at just the same spot. The vessel was assisted off and into harbour the following day.

On October 2nd, 1858 there was an adjudication on the case of the Pandarves of St Ives heading from Sheids for Exmouth, Loaded with coal ran aground on Holm Sands on Friday 24th at 10am. At the Court house before Chas Steward Esq, presiding, the salvors, Robert Hook and others where represented by Mr. W.R.Seago, and the ship by Mr.Small, Lloyds agent. It appeared that the master having gotten the ship grounded employed the salvors at about 8pm, when they shortly after got her off, brought her through the channel, and safety moored her in the roads about 1am Saturday, making little or no water. The court having complimented Hook on the straight forward manner in which he gave evidence, awarded the salvors £36, and costs £5 15s 6d.

On Sat 30th October 1858 it was reported in the press of an Accident at Sea. -On Sunday morning William Brown, one of the crew of the fishing boat "Red Rover," Robert Hook master, William Rose, owner, was conveyed to Lowestoft infirmary, having sustained an injury to his eye. When the boat was outside the Sands, a boy was sent below to fetch the gun for one of the crew to shoot at a gull; bringing the gun up it when off and injured Brown, who was sleeping on the deck, in the eye. We hear that no shot struck him, or it would have been serious. In connection with the lifeboat the following story followed; On Tuesday evening a youth named Robert Thaine, whose parents live in Mariners-street, fell off the new lifeboat shed which is now being erected. He was found by Dr.Wardleworth in an insensible state, with a large scalp wound behind the right ear, extending to the bone. He was taken to a cottage, and subsequently home, and is, we hear, doing well.

On the 25th December 1858, Robert had drawn the short straw and was on lookout, the wind was blowing W.S.W., clear, moderate weather, when he witnessed the following. The brig "Peggy," Captain F.A.Le'Breton, from Sunderland, of and for Jersey, with coals, was at anchor being it was Christmas Day, when a screw steamer called the "Neptune," of Sunderland, laden and bound South ran into her mid-ships on the starboard side, cutting away covering boards, staving nine planks, breaking timbers, and doing considerable other damage. The steamer passed on rendering no assistance what-so-ever. Hook while this was happening launched the yawl "I'LL Try," with 19 men and came alongside, the captain refused to employ them, but requested them to go after the screw steamer and ascertain her name, which was found to be the Neptune, of Sunderland. Later on that day the Old Company did assist the French lugger, "Mariquita," Henry, master, from Sunderland, for Redan, with coals, off the Newcome Sand. On the following Wednesday an adjudication Case was heard by Charles steward and Mr. Leathes., who awarded the sum of £15. The vessel to pay costs of £5, the chairman remarked that the salvors ran no risk, as the water was still and weather fine. This did not appear to satisfy the salvors, who are stated to have asked £80. For the service rendered.

Admiralty Court. -Friday. Before Dr.Lushington, Lowestoft Beach-men V the Brig "Come. On". This was a claim made by the Old Company of beach-men, for a reward for salvage services rendered to the brig "Come-On", of Sunderland, on the 21st January 1859. It appears that the brig in the course of her voyage from Sunderland, coal laden, for Porto-Rigo, grounded on the Newcome-Sand, and the salvors, my means of laying out the stern anchor and 80 fathoms of 5in chain, and heaving thereon, succeeded in getting her off. They worked at the pumps, and the ship was ultimately laid on the mud near the graving dock, Lowestoft. The owners contested that it was a trivial service. It was agreed that the value of the property salved was £2098. Dr.Swabey appeared for the salvors; Dr.Twiss, Q.C., and Dr.Adams, Q.C., for the owners. Dr.Lushington delivered the following judgment.- This ship on the 21st of January got on the Newcome Sand, in the immediate neighbour-hood of Lowestoft, and there cannot be a doubt that it was a work of some difficulty to remove her from that situation of some peril. She was removed by the assistance of these persons, who represent themselves as salvors, and who brought her into a place of safety. The service was a short one and simple. The principal ingredient is the danger the ship was in by remaining on the sand, and the danger to which she might have been exposed had the wind and weather changed. I leave out of consideration entirely the agreement, because there was no agreement between the parties at all. An offer was made to them of £50, which was not accepted. The question is what the court ought to give. I consider £100 is quite sufficient for all that was done. I see no reason why the case might not have been settled on the spot, and certainly I see no reason whatever why the court should certify that this is a proper case to be brought before the High Court of Admiralty, and therefore I shall award £100, but no costs.

On February 15th, 1859 the brig "Diana", of Newcastle, grounded on the Holm Sand, about 9am. The Lowestoft Companies-known as the Old and the Young's Companies-immediately launched their yawls and proceeded to her assistance. The Youngs yawl was first to the vessel, when, according to rule, Hook in the Old Company yawl returned to shore.

The next day the 16th in the afternoon the steam-tug was engaged in its legitimate calling of towing vessels into Lowestoft Harbour, and while so employed a collision took place in the Stanford channel, between two brigs, the "Governor", of Sunderland, and another, when the Lowestoft Boat Companies again launched their yawls, and proceeded to the vessels. The Old Company's yawl "Happy new year", was the first to board the brig "Governor", when the Youngs Company yawl "Young prince" returned to shore. The salvors offered to make agreement to assist the brig into Lowestoft Harbour, for the sum of £35. The steam-tug also seeing the collision, left her own work, although there were seven or eight vessels with burgees flying, requiring her to tow them into harbour, and proceeded to the brig and took her in tow, and thus again unfairly preventing the service of Hook and his fellow salvors from being accepted.

On Feb 25th, 1859 the beach-men of both Lowestoft and Pakefield salvage yawl and boat companies, waited upon the magistrate for their advice and at the same time submitted a complaint to the board of trade. It was observed that the beach-men of both towns were of the opinion that the steam-tug was unfairly interfering with their salvage employment. On several occasions the steam tug had unjustly deprived them of cases of salvage, and the minds of the men have been considerably irritated in consequence, they were strongly commended in taking this action and not for taking the law in their own hands. It was stated at the time that all three companies had a standing rule between them that whichever company's boats first reached the vessel requiring assistance the competing companies would retire and leave the first boat in possession. The findings were that the steam tug belonging to the Eastern Counties Railway Company, unfairly interfered with their (the beachmans) employment and cited three cases in proof: one of which occurred on the 15th February, in which the two Lowestoft Companies had proceeded to the assistance of the "Diana" on holm sands, when according to the rule, the second boat returned to shore and after 8 hours laying alongside the steam tug went off and refloated her and towed her to harbour. The outcome was that Lowestoft had a fully manned lifeboat in hours of need and was not the job of the steam tug. Hook stated "We do not object to the steam-tugs going off to render salvage services to vessels in all cases for which they may be signalled; nor do we object to their having the preference in all cases in which the steam-tug is the first to board or offer assistance. We only ask and desire that there should be the same understanding between ourselves and the steam-tugs as is now existing between our three Beach Companies". Robert went on to say, "We humbly pray that your honourable board will use your best influence with the Eastern Counties Railway Company for the bringing about a proper understanding on the subject matter of this petition". They went on to report how Hooks crew had saved 33 persons from a watery grave that winter.

On Friday 8th April 1859, the brig "Commerce", Young, of Lynn, from Newcastle, for Rotterdam, with coke and chains, grounded on the North part of the Holm-Sand, filled with water, and sank in the course of the night. Robert who was on look-out immediately raised the alarm, and with four other members of the company took a yawl to rescue the in-peril crew. Landing the water-lodged crew at Lowestoft and they were forwarded home on the next day, by the honorary agent of the ship-wrecked mariners society, W. Cole. Esq. The Old Company saved her rigging etc, and employed a driving cutter to recover her cargo of chains.

On Wednesday 11th May 1859, Robert and fellow Lifeboat members attended the opening of the new Lifeboat House. The National Lifeboat Institution had just built on this important station, a new house for the Lowestoft Lifeboat. It was a substantial commodious building in every way. Its cost was £160, the amount of which was with the exception of £52, had been paid by the National Lifeboat Institution.

On Sunday 31st July 1859, the schooner "Catherine and Mary," Robert, of Port Madoe, from Pelew for London, was assisted off the Holm-Sand by the old company, and afterwards into harbour by the harbour company's tug "powerful." The salvors were agreed with for £200, and the tug for £8 for their respective services.

The anniversary of the Suffolk Humane Society and Lowestoft Lifeboat association was held on Tuesday 30th August 1859, when the Lowestoft and Pakefield Lifeboat were afloat for the inspection of the subscribers and the public, and took their accustomed trip to seaward, each having on board a number of visitors. On this occasion Robert had arranged for a group of children from the local beach village school to accompany them on the trip. The boats made their appearance in the outer harbour shortly after eleven o'clock, from whence they sailed in a southerly direction round the Holm Head, and then stood for the harbour, where they arrived shortly after twelve o'clock, and the company was disembarked at the respective landing piers, most were in fine spirits apart from a few children who were a bit green around the gills. The latter may have been due to the sea being rough with a stiff breeze from the south-west., there was an excellent opportunity of testing the capabilities of these first-class boats.

Pier Head, Lowestoft

About 8a.m. on Thursday, the 8th September 1859, the French schooner "Auguste Marie", Maurouard, of and for Dieppe, from Newcastle, grounded on Holm Sand, and has since become a wreck. Alarm rockets were sent up from the "Stanford" light ship, in answer to which the beach-men including Hook of the Old Company, went off, and brought the crew (5 hands) ashore. The name board of this vessel adorned the outside of the Old Company shed for over half a century.

On Wednesday Oct 5th, 1859 there was an, Adjudication in the case of the French brig "Reine Hortense" Captain Allaire, of Nantes for Newcastle which beached and grounded on Holm-Sands, about noon of Thursday the 29th. The case was heard before Charles Steward and Robert Cook Fowler Esqs, at the court house. Mr. Seago appeared for the salvors, Robert Hook and John Mewse, and their comrades in the Old Beach company; Mr. Small who was the French Vice -Consul at Lowestoft, represented the vessel, which he stated to be 4 years old and an agreed value of £1500.The statement made by Mr. Seago on behalf of his clients was read out as follows:- Robert Hook who was on watch observed the above vessel coming in from sea, and not long after she struck upon the sands; upon which they launched their yawl "Mutquito" and the band of twelve proceeded off, and on getting on side Hook enquired of the captain, "Do you have an anchor laid"? The captain replied, " I Want the French Consul" and Upon hearing this the crew returned to shore to collect Mr. Small, but found his assistant Mr. Cordingiey, then after rowing back to the beached vessel Mr. Cordingiey went aboard to speak to the Captain, having had a conversation with the Captain, he wished the salvors at once to go to work and get the vessel into safety. Leaving the matter to be settled by the local magistrates. To this proposition the salvors demurred, thinking their services might be of greater value than the maximum sum (£200) that could be awarded by the magistrates: under the Merchant Shipping Act. The weather having become finer, the salvors offered their services for £180, which the Captain declined giving; upon which an agreement was entered into, and the matter left for the local adjudicators. The salvors then went to work, laid the kedge and two warps to an end, by which time their large yawl, "Princess Royal," with twenty four hands came off, into which 100 fathems of chain was passed, and then the tide served the bow anchor (1, 1/2cwt).This with the help of the kedge and warps, and the yawls anchor and cables, was hauled out & laid, and about 10pm the vessel came and was towed into the South Road and anchored north of the harbour about 11pm with the action starting at 5pm. The next morning the salvors assisted her into the inner harbour and she was safely moored near the graving dock. The court heard from Mr. Small who stated he had no further comment other than to speak in terms of the highest commendation of the quiet and straight forward conduct of Hook and his men. He hoped Hook would continue as their leader, and he was sure the magistrates would make their award to the agreement to the rule. The chairman (Mr. steward) observed that the vessel when taken hold of by the steam tug was not in distress or difficulties, she had been anchored in the roads and riding there all night; all the damage and difficulty was over, and he could not see that more than the ordinary rate could be asked. The Chairman remarked, that having considered the case they had awarded £120, the ship paying the costs of £5.15shillings. Addressing Hook, he observed," I am glad you have behaved like good fellows, as you always do when you are in proper humour, sometimes you get it a little wrong, but you generally work round."

Later on, in the day on Thursday 29th September 1859, a French brig grounded upon the Holm-Sand, and remained till the evening flood, when she was got off by Robert and the Old Company of beach-men.

On the 9th October 1859, the sloop "Dove," Silvester, from headley for London, with coals, was assisted off the Holm-Sand by Hook and fellow beach-men of the old company.

On the 26th October 1859 early in the morning a Schooner named the Lord Douglas from Dundee sailing from Bowness for Doit with pig iron, was driven by the South-West gale's onto Corton Beach. The coastguard attempted to reach her with a line using a rocket apparatus, but after a number of try's they sent for the lifeboat, Robert hook gathered his crew and made off to Corton, arriving at the schooner or what was left, they found the crew alive and hanging from the exposed rigging and having cast a line the crew were pulled aboard. Just as they were about to leave Hook noted he could hear a bell ringing in between the noise of the crashing waves but as the foresail had split during this rescue it would be pointless attempting another rescue till it was replaced. Putting ashore, beaching the Lifeboat opposite the Warren House, Hook ran ahead to the boatshed for a replacement foresail after leaving half the Lifeboat crew with the boat and the other half to walk the five rescued men back to the Boat house. Having returned with a replacement sail and fresh crew members they set back out to Corton bank, the Schooner Silva from Glasgow had been riding out the gale anchored by Holm sand, but she parted from her anchor and was driven on to the Corton bank. By this time the Pakefield lifeboat had been sent for and was neck and neck in the race to reach the Silva but she over shot the mark, but Hook was more successful and, having come to windward, through the heavy breakers he reached her. After getting off the crew of four, yet another Schooner was seen in distress, but the replacement foresail had split again by the violence of the gale. The Lowestoft boat made for Yarmouth and the Pakefield boat aided the schooner. Once landing in Yarmouth the Silva's crew were handed to the Shipwrecked Fisherman Society, were they were duly supplied with dry clothes, food etc. The National Lifeboat Institution subsequently voted both crews £100 for their valuable exertions during these storms.

On Friday 28th October late in the evening the brig "Panope", Weetman, master, of and from Sunderland, for London, with coal, struck upon the Holm Sand. The Old Company of beach-men went to her assistance, and on the following morning she was conducted into the Harbour by the company's tug "Imperial". The Salvors received £80 for their services. On the same night the brig "Percy", of and from Sunderland, also for London, with coal, also struck on the Holm Sand. The Old Company also went to her assistance, and agreed to get her off and into a place of safety for £200. The weather came on very bad, and the salvors and crew left her about 11pm. Early the next morning when Hook and company boarded the vessel, they found five feet of water in her. Pumps were set to work, and sails set on the vessel, and she was forced over the sand, when, with the assistance of the steam-tug, she was towed into Lowestoft Harbour.

On Friday 5th November 1859 it was reported in the paper of a hurricane from the west-south-west hitting the coast of Lowestoft making for a most thrilling and exciting day for the beach-men. A statement was made, described back then from the brave and noble beach-men to the Suffolk Humane Society. It was Tuesday about 11am, the wind was blowing west-south-west, with a heavy sea from the roadstead, when they observed a screw steam ship (which afterwards proved to be the "Shamrock", of Dublin, Captain Donn) coming in from the southward, and they were certain unless her course was altered she would ground on the holm head. Which she shortly after did, beating heavily, they raised a flag of distress up the rigging. They at once ran to their Lifeboat, and with the assistance of 100 hands launched her with great difficulty through the heavy surf on the beach. They immediately proceeded to the ship, and in crossing the Newcome Sand experienced a dreadful sea, which broke several times over the boat, filling her with water. On approaching the Shamrock, the crew on board her waved them on, and were replied to by the coxswain Robert. Hook, "We'll be with you directly my lads, only look out to catch the rope". Having dropped anchor a line was thrown on board, and afterwards a second, to keep the boat into position, and by this means the crew which numbered fourteen were hauled a distance of thirty yards through the breakers to the Lifeboat. The last man, the Captain having been rescued, they made for the beach where they landed them at about one pm, amist the acclamation of hundreds of spectators.

It was noted at the time spectators from Wellington Terrace to the high light house witnessed Robert Hook and his crew in their gallant rescue on their mission of mercy. Great was the excitement on shore when the Lifeboat returned to the beach and the spectators saw, one by one, the ship's crew take the fearful leap into the surging foaming breakers to return to dry land. There were shouts of applause by the onlookers as the Lifeboat crew came ashore with their appreciation of the crew's gallantry.

On Wednesday the following week after the Shamrock rescue the Suffolk Humane Society Committee and the Lowestoft and Pakefield Lifeboat Association held a meeting at the Court House, Charles. Steward, Esq., presiding. Captain Joachim having reported on the inefficient state of the Lowestoft Lifeboat sails, a new suit was ordered. An order was also given for half-a-dozen suits of clothes for the use of shipwrecked men, from the shipwrecked Seaman's Fund connected with the institution. Robert Hook the coxswain of the Lowestoft Lifeboat attended and reported the saving of the crew of the two vessels noticed the previous week and also that of the Shamrock.

RESCUE OF THE CREW OF THE STEAMER "SHAMROCK," OF DUBLIN, BY THE LOWESTOFT LIFE-BOAT.

The Committee promised to represent these cases, and especially that of the Shamrock, to the notice of the Board of Trade and the Royal National Lifeboat Institution. If ever gallant services deserved to be rewarded with a medal, those rendered to the Shamrock must be classed with them, and they hoped the recommendation of the committee would succeed in obtaining for them this mark of approval, of which the men would be greatly proud. On the 12th November 1859, the schooner "Hannah," Harvey, of Colchester, was towed out of harbour in ballast, for the North. Soon after the steam-tug cast off it was found that the schooner was making a great deal of water, which compelled the crew to run her for the beach, where it was discovered that she had pricked herself with her anchor. An agreement was made with Robert Hook and his fellow old company men to get her off, which they succeeded in doing that night, when she was towed into the harbour by the steam-tug. The salvors received £50 for their services.

Suffolk Humane Society. -At a packed meeting of the committee of the Suffolk Humane Society, held on Wednesday 16th November 1859, at the Court-house, Charles. Steward, Esq., in the chair, Captain Joachim, R.N., handed in a letter which he had received from Mr. Lucas, Secretary to the Royal National Lifeboat institution, from which it appears that the sum of £67.10s had been forwarded for distribution to the crews of the Pakefield and Lowestoft lifeboats, as follows:- Lowestoft lifeboat, for services to the Silva, wrecked on Corton Sands, £14.10s; Lowestoft Lifeboat, for services to the Lord Douglas, wrecked on Corton beach, £14.10s.; Pakefield lifeboat, for services to the French schooner La Jeane Mathilde, wrecked opposite the Royal Hotel, £24 (night-work). The Lowestoft men were informed that their gallant services to the Shamrock, in saving 14 hands, were under the consideration of the committee in London. Coxswain Robert Hook, thanked the committee on behalf of his crew.

On Sunday November 27th, 1859, the schooner "Lord Strangford," of Guernsey, for St Malo, with coals, struck upon the Holm-Sand about 6 a.m., and was assisted off by Hook and the beach-men of the Old Company. They were to receive £120 for their services.

On Friday 9th December, Robert and his fellow Old Company beach-men received a fine new yawl, named the "Bittern". She was 51 feet in length, built by Messrs. Mack and Jermyn, of South-town, at a cost of upwards of £140. Her owners expected she would be the fastest boat along the coast, and she would be successful in all her pursuits.

On Saturday 10th December 1859, "Brittern" got her first chance to prove her worth, the schooner "Earl of Devon", Dusting, master, of Penzance, for Liverpool, with wheat, was assisted off the Newcome Sand and into harbour by the Old Company of beach-men. A claim of £400 had been made for the service rendered, which was not entertained and was due to be heard in court.

On the Wednesday 21st December 1859, the barque "Eva," Mills, of and from Dundee, for Valparaiso, with coals attempted to take the harbour at low water without a pilot or any signal for assistance, and as a consequence grounded and struck the pier heads, and knocked away her bowsprit, figure head, and received other damage as well as damaging the pier. With assistance of the harbour pilot, our beach-men of the Old Company, and the steam-tug, as the water flowed she was removed from her position to within the pier-heads, after beating heavily and making some water. The next day she was assisted into the inner harbour, and discharged her cargo. Within a week she was wrecked at Harwich and her figure head, days after she left Lowestoft appeared displayed on the Old Company shed. The salvage services rendered to the above schooner were settled for, by private arrangement, at £350. The ship was valued at £285, and the cargo at £1832.10s. The £350 was apportioned between the Lifeboat crew, steam-tug, and the beach-men.

On Christmas Eve 1859, Mr.Bradbeer, ship agent, at Lowestoft, settled with the beach-man of the Old Company, for their services rendered to the "Earl of Devon", of Penzance, Wheat laden, for the sum of £200. The men did ask for £400. Robert Hook was reported to say: - "It is an ill wind that blows no one good, and we are glad, on the account of many of our aged beach-men, who came in for the doles on this occasion, that this case has been settled so opportunely for Christmas". "But for this, some of the poor folks would have come rather short at this time of our National feasting."

On the 27th December 1859, the schooner "Babthorpe", Thos. Royal, of Hull, from Kircaldy, for Trieste, with coals, about 7.30 a.m., grounded on the South-West edge of the

Newcome Sand, where she beat heavily. She was assisted off at about 3 p.m., by the beach-men of the Old Company and into the roadstead under agreement for £160, which was paid by Mr.B.M.Bradbeer, agent for the vessel.

On December 28th, 1859 the Royal National Lifeboat Institution, in connection with the Suffolk Humane Society and Lowestoft and Pakefield Lifeboat Association held a public meeting at the Court House. The Chairman called upon Captain Joachim to read the letter which he had received from the secretary of the Royal National Lifeboat Institution, and which accompanied the silver medals and votes of thanks, on parchment.

LIFE-BOAT MEDAL.

The following brave fellows named there in; Robert Hook,

Francis Smith, Richard Butcher, Thomas Liffen, Alfred Mewse, James Butcher, and William Rose, all the Lowestoft Lifeboat, and Nathaniel Colby, Coxswain of the Pakefield Lifeboat. The letter having been read, the chairman then presented them in the above order, the Society's Silver Breast medal, enclosed in a neat morocco case, and the vote of thanks on parchment, in an appropriate rose wood frame, and having done which, he proceeded to say "Perhaps it is better that i should explain to you that our Suffolk Humane Society has for the last two years, acted in concert with the Royal National Lifeboat Institution, the former finding the boats and their gear, and the latter the ways and means of rewarding the men for their gallant and mediatory services."(Hear Hear) from the public gallery, the chairman carried on to say, "That the society is supported by voluntary contributions throughout the whole of this great country."(Cheers from the public gallery)"As a National Society it has for its head our good, gracious, and beloved Queen; and on the list of its contributors are very many of the most distinguished countrymen",(Hear Hear from the gallery)"and now to my men(addressing himself to the hardy beach-men) these medals and votes of thanks, which are on parchment, are presented to you by the Royal National Lifeboat Institution, for your very meritorious services in rescuing lives from shipwreck, during the late terrible and disastrous storms with which we were visited in the months of October and November last". "I think i may say that you may wear these medals with the same proud feeling with which many other of your countrymen are now wearing the

Victoria Cross".(loud cheers from the Public Gallery)" You certainly have by your skill in your boats, your perseverance, your defiance of danger, your love of humanity, saved many lives from a watery grave, and this you have done certainly at the immediate risk of your own lives, i cannot ask for more"(The Public gallery stands and cheers.)

NATHANIEL COLBY, COXSWAIN OF THE PAKEFIELD LIFE-BOAT.

 On 30th December 1859, the Spanish brig, "Trinidad," of and for Sunderland from Christiansund, with Deal and Codfish, grounded upon the Holm-Sand, and soon sank. The Old Company saved the crew in their yawl, and had been sent home by Mr.Preston, of Yarmouth, the Spanish Vice-Consul at that port. The Old Company displayed the "Trinidad" name board on their shed like a trophy.

On the 31st January 1860, the barque "Ring Mason Castle," Corey, of Jersey, from Hartlepool, for Plymouth, with coals, making water, having sprung a leak, assisted in by Old Company beach-men for £30.

The "Scynthia Ann" brig, Ridley, of London, from Sunderland, grounded on the North-end of the Newcome Sand, at about midnight, on Saturday 3rd March 1860, and was assisted into harbour at about 2 a.m., by the Old Company making no water. Settled with for £20, by Mr.B.M.Bradbeer, ship-agent.

On the 9th April 1860, the schooner "William," Garnsworth, master, from Hartlepool, of and for Exeter, with coals, grounded upon newcome about 4 p.m., and was assisted off by Hook and fellow beach-men, and into the harbour about 9 p.m.- on the 10th.

On the 22nd April 1860, the brig "Miriam," Naylor, from London, of and for Hartlepool, struck on the Newcome-sand about noon, and was assisted off by the old beach company, by agreement for £20, which was paid by Mr.B.M.Bradbeer.

On the 13th May 1860, the schooner "Ann," Merren, of North Shields, for London, struck upon the Holm-Sand, about 10 a.m., and was assisted off by the Old Beach Company, about 4. p.m., under agreement for £110, which has been paid by Mr.B.M.Bradbeer, ship agent. She proceeded, making no water.

On Sunday 28th May 1860, the wind was very high, but during the night and most of Monday, it blew a perfect hurricane from the West. North. West., when the Lowestoft roadstead was, what mariners term, all a spoon-drift. The Pakefield, Kessingland and Lowestoft Lifeboats, - were all out on service, the latter of which brought ashore two water-logged crews. One from the brig "Rapid," of Portsmouth; and the other, consisting of the master, his wife, daughter, son and an infant of eleven months old, from the sloop "Three Brothers," of Goole, loaded with bones from London to Stockworth, the mate "William Barley" however who attempted to jump on board a schooner the sloop had run into, was drowned. The above sloop was being towed by a tug and was pulled over the anchor chain of a schooner, which caused it to lose her rudder and bowsprit, and became unmanageable. All were landed at Lowestoft by Hook and his gallant crew. The poor creatures were taken in by Mrs. Neane, on Lowestoft beach village, and their wants supplied from a private fund, the master not belonging to the shipwrecked mariner's society. The master told the local press, he never expected to have been saved, but his wife with tears said-" I had faith in the Lord that we should not find a watery grave, and he sent our saviour's Robert Hook and his skill-full Lifeboat crew."

On Monday 29th May 1860, the "Scotia," Henderson, From Sunderland for London grounded on the Newcome Sand. Robert immediately launched the Lifeboat, took off the crew and at high water the Yarmouth steam-tug "Volunteer," pulled her off, where she was anchored in the North-Roads.

On the 22nd June 1860, the Prussian schooner "Otto August," Maas, of and from Stralsund, for London, with wheat, assisted off the Holm-Sand by Old Company beach-men, at about 11p.m., making little or no water. The sum of £350 was paid for the services rendered. Supposed value of the ship's cargo was £2,400.

On the 15th July 1860, the French schooner "Georges Emile," Captain Bernier, of Nantes, from Caen, for Sunderland, in ballast, grounded on the Holm-Sand, and was assisted off and into harbour by the Old Beach Company at 6 p.m. This case was settled by Captain. Small, French Vice-Consul, for £55.

On the 12th August 1860, the "Northumberland" (Steam-Ship), Roberts, From Newcastle for London, with coals, grounded on the north part of the Newcome-Sand, about 10.30 a.m., the old beach company laid an anchor by agreement for £100 for the tide, but she did not come off on the flood. Part of the cargo was then thrown over by the crew, who succeeded in getting her off about 5 a.m., the next morning, when she anchored in the roads, and afterwards proceeded. The beach-men where settled with by Capt. Small for £102.10s.

On Monday 20th August 1860, the Suffolk Humane Society and Lowestoft Lifeboat Association and celebrated its anniversary of this excellent institution. In the morning both the Lowestoft and Pakefield Lifeboats were afloat for the inspection of its subscribers and the public, and took their accustomed trip to seaward, each having on board a number of pleasure-seeking friends. On board both boats was also the band of St. Marks School, Windsor, who were staying at Pakefield, through the kindness of the Rev.T.Hawtrey. The boats sailed from the harbour shortly after eleven o'clock in a southerly direction as far as Pakefield lightship, and then back again to the harbour, where they arrived between twelve and one o'clock. Both boats were found to be in excellent working order and condition. On their return Manby's apparatus for effecting communication with stranded vessels was exhibited on the south pier. A line from the mortar was thrown from the South over the North pier, and the necessary running gear having been fixed, a lad was drawn in from one pier to the other, in birt's cork life buoy, in order to give a practical proof to the hundreds of visitors who crowded the pier. To the great amusement of the company, the lad, from the hawser slacking, received quite a ducking. Experiments were also tried with Denne's rockets, which startled many of the ladies.

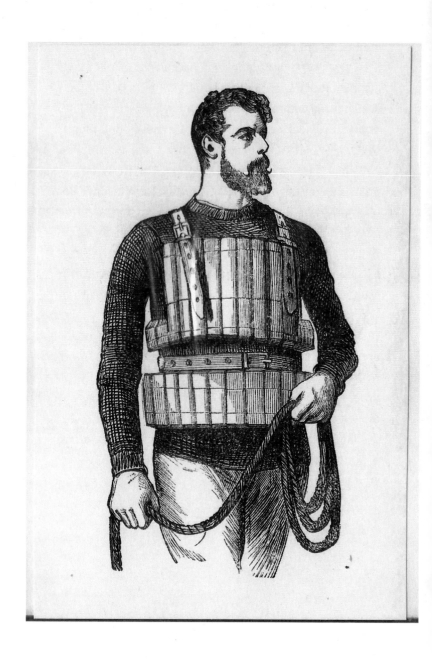

On Saturday 1st September 1860, the sloop "Luna," proudly, of goole, from London for stockwith, with bones, was assisted off the Newcome-Sand by the old beach company, and into harbour, making water, by agreement, for £60.

The brig "Hero of Kars," Macfie, of Glasgow, from Shield, for Alexandria, with coals, struck on the inner shoal on Saturday 22nd September 1860, and was assisted off without damage, by Hook and the Old Beach Company for £15.

The French schooner "Marie Alexandrine", of Nantes, from Newcastle, for Nantes, with coals, grounded on the Holm Sand on Monday 8th October 1860. The Old Beach Company boarded her, and were subsequently employed to get them off. Having laid an anchor, Robert proceeded to go back to shore, leaving two company members on board, intending to go back on her with 10 hands to heave on the anchor chain on the flood tide at 3.a.m., Tuesday morning. Accordingly, about midnight Robert and Company returned to her, but found she had, with the assistance of part of the crew of a French barque, riding in Corton Roads, succeeded in getting her off, and had anchored her in the roads. The two Beach-men who had remained on board were forced off by the French crew, when on the flood tide, she proceeded out of the Stanford Channel, thus leaving the salvors and Hook unsettled with. The men having taken legal advice, proceeded with their yawl and the tug having on board the collector of customs, armed with his warrant, out of Pakefield gat, with the view of cutting her off and arresting her. The French Captain observing them in pursuit, immediately sent his hands aloft to make full sail. By this time Hook had got his yawl a full League (about three miles) off the coast and consequently was without the legal limit for arresting her progress. The parties after an exciting trip returned to land. The Old Company would presume legal proceeding through the French authorities.

On Monday 15th October 1860, the brig "Grange," Thomas Wood, of Scarborough, from Hartlepool for London, with a crew of eight hands, arrived off Southwold about noon of Monday, and due to the bad weather put back for shelter in Yarmouth Roads; and about 3.p.m., owing to the wind increasing and the rain being so thick as to obscure the buoys, struck upon Corton Sand. There being too much sea to do anything with their own boat, a signal was made for assistance, when Robert Hook saw the signal and set out in a yawl with other members of the Old Beach Company, and laid out a kedge warp, but were unable from the violence of the sea to get out the bower anchor. The vessel commencing to break up, Hook threw out a rope, the crew were compelled to abandon her and made for the yawl, and were landed upon our beach at about 9p.m., in a destitute state, saving little more than the clothes they stood in. The vessel was a total wreck. The above crew was forwarded home by the Shipwrecked Mariners Society.

On Sunday 10th March 1861, about 4p.m., the brig "Le Guiletta," Fulcher, from Grimsby, of and for London, with coals, got upon the Holm-Sand, and was assisted off by the Old Company beach-men and anchored in the roads about

8p.m.

On the 22nd March 1861, the barque "Euphrates", White, of and from Sunderland, for London, in ballast, got upon the Newcome-Sand, about 10a.m. She was assisted off by Robert and his fellow members of the Old Company, and anchored in the South-roads at about 3p.m. An agreement was made for £85, which was paid by Messrs. Gowing and Co., to the salvors.

The barque "Eslington," of South Shields, from Antwerp, for Lowestoft grounded on the Newcome Sand on Monday 1st April 1861. Robert who was on lookout that night raised the alarm and took a yawl to the barque, and an agreement was made to get her off and anchored in the roads.

On the 22nd April 1861, the Danish sloop "Marianne," Hansen, of Svendbury, from Ipswich for Hartlepool, with ballast, having been assisted off the Newcome Sand by the beach-men of the old company. Their services were settled for by Mr.B.M.Bradbeer for £55.

On Tuesday 7th May 1861, the brig "Robert & Mary", Young, of and for Blythe from Roven, in ballast, grounded on the Newcome Sand about noon, as did also the brig "Asia", Miller, Of Seaham, from Hamburg for Sunderland, in ballast. Both vessels were assisted off by the Old Company, about 3 a.m., and both then anchored in the South-Roads. The salvors were settled with by Messrs. Gowing and Co., receiving for the "Robert & Mary", £60, and for the "Asia",

£90.

On Monday 13th May 1861, the brig "Sarah Bell," Mugridge, of Arundel, from Little Hampton, for the North, grounded upon the Newcome Sand about 3 p.m., and was assisted off about 8 p.m., by Robert Hook and his fellow old company beach-men, by agreement, for £35, which was paid by Mr.B.M.Bradbeer, ship agent. On the following Saturday, the schooner "Raven," Fearn, of and from Whitstable, for Hartlepool, in ballast, came upon the Ness-point, and again assisted off on Sunday by the old beach company, who have been settled with by Mr.Bradbeer, for £50.

On Thursday morning at about 11a.m, on the 25th July 1861, it was blowing a gale of wind from the S.S.W., a brig, waiting out the storm in the Lowestoft roads, ran into the Holm-Sands. The Lowestoft Lifeboat in connection with the R.N.L.I., was immediately launched, and proceeded to the rescue of the shipwrecked crew. Having succeeded in closing in on the vessel, the Lifeboat saved all eight hands. The sea broke heavily over the brig during the time it took to rescue the crew; but Hook skillfully managed the Lifeboat, and fortunately no loss of life. The Lifeboat lost her anchor and incurred slight damage. The brig proved to be French, the "St Michael," with a cargo of deal from Christiana to Marans. The sailors were handed over to the French agent at Lowestoft and then to the sailor's home for a change of clothes and a warm meal.

The Anniversary of the Suffolk Humane Society, and the

Lowestoft and Pakefield Lifeboat Association was celebrated on Friday 9th August 1861, when the Pakefield and Lowestoft Lifeboats, the new Pakefield new surf Lifeboat, and lastly the harbour company's boat were afloat, for the inspection of the subscribers and the public, and took their accustomed trip to seaward, each having on board a number of pleasure-seeking friends. At eleven o'clock the boats left the harbour and proceeded as far as the cage-buoy, off the Barnard Sand, and from thence back to the harbour, where they arrived between twelve and one o'clock. All four boats were reported to be in excellent condition, and fit for immediate service. The Manby's apparatus for effecting communication with stranded vessels was then demonstrated. The line was thrown from the South to the North pier, and a man passed backwards and forwards in order to give practical proof of the manner in which persons are rescued from vessels in distress. During the time the boats were exercised, a French brig struck on the Newcome Sand; the Lowestoft and Pakefield boats being nearest hastened to offer assistance, and a man from the Pakefield boat attempted to get on board, when the master of the French vessel, frightened at their officious kindness, met him and threw and threw him back into the Lifeboat: fortunately, he received no serious injury. The committee afterwards adjourned to the Royal Hotel, and audited the annual accounts, and made awards for saving life and other acts of humanity which had been performed during the past year.

This fashionable watering- place has for many years been

celebrated for its marine fetes, which, at times, have rivalled in character and interest those of more general renown. We have, however, like the vast water which spread their expansive bosom north, east, and south of us, and which now ripple their soft music in strains among the pebbles, and anon dash in angry roar upon our beach been subject to the law of ebb and flow. 1860 was one of catastrophe and distress, its fearful gales carried dismay into many a family, and the almost unprecedented wetness of the season cast dampness and gloom around, and cut off the demand for those amusements which were so much in request when fine weather obtains. As a consequence, the ebb set in, and Lowestoft had no regatta. This season, we are happy to say, the tide has turned, the flood has made; and with weather the most brilliant, with Lowestoft full to overflowing with visitors, and with every heart gladdened by the prospect of an abundant harvest, it was only what was expected that efforts should be made for renewing those healthful and exhilarating amusements which our roadstead regattas have always afforded. The day fixed for the regatta was Thursday the 29th August 1861, when the weather was all that could possibly be desired, the clouds forming a grateful shade from the scorching rays of the sun, and a brisk breeze from the north- west aiding materially the sailing contests. On proceeding down London- Road to the south pier, you could have observed a rich display of bunting from the Royal and Suffolk Hotels, Fish-market, Harbour masters grounds, and the various consulate offices etc. At the end of the pier was a raised platform for the use of the umpires- Charles Steward, and R.C. Fowler. Esq - and the committee, and where also the representatives of the press were accommodated. Moored opposite the pier was the schooner "Eliza," the flag ship from whence the various signals where fired. On the centre of the pier was located the band of the 10th Hussars, which, by permission of colonel baker and offices, performed a choice selection of music in beautiful style. The Norfolk Militia Artillery band performed on the Battery- Green. Throughout the day the South and North piers, Esplanades, Beach north and south, were thickly studded with pleasure seekers. The South pier was crowded by a most fashionable assemblage. The first race of the day was by that splendid and useful class of boat, the yawls, for a purse of 25 Sovereigns. Half a minute per foot being allowed for difference of length. The first place £13, the second £8, and the 3rd £4, with no entrance fee. For this interesting match the following entered: - Bittern, Robert Hook, 50 feet, Lowestoft; Musquito, James Ayres, 44 feet, Lowestoft; Eclipse, William Bobbitt, 54 feet, Lowestoft; Thought, William Capps, 49 feet, Lowestoft. The course for these was from mooring opposite the pier north to the flag boat at the Ness-Point, thence to the Stanford light ship up the channel, crossing the Newcome to a flag- boat opposite Pakefield, thence to the starting point. To sail round the course three times, total distance about 21 miles. On the signal being given for them to take their station, considerable interest was excited as they proceeded out of harbour to their moorings. At one o'clock the signal was fired for starting, when in the twinkling of an eye up went a cloud of canvass, and all got away pretty well together, dancing to a stiff breeze from the North- West. Eclipse taking the lead, followed by musquito, thought, and bittern. On rounding the Stanford lightship, the Thought was considered to take the lead, but did not long maintain it. The splendid sailing of these boats was greatly admired. Their times of coming in were as follows: - Eclipse, Thought, Bittern and Musquito gave up after one lap.

THE LOWESTOFT REGATTA.—DRAWN BY DUNCAN.

On Saturday 2nd November 1861, "Last night," says Robert. Hook, Lowestoft coxswain "It was blowing such a heavy gale from the North with a sea beating hard agaisnt the harbour mouth. At about 10p.m., I witnessed a signal of distress in the direction of the Ness-point, when I decided to man and launch the Lifeboat through a tremendous surf. We stood northward, and we discovered the schooner by her repeating her signals of distress, and, having hailed her, found the crew were not able to keep her afloat. We closed on her and I threw nine hands on board, which enabled us to slip their cable and run for the harbour." Captain Joachim R.N., expressed great pleasure in hearing testimony to the usual courage of the Lifeboat's crew, and Hook's skillful management of the boat on this occasion in a heavy gale and pitch-black night. The vessel proved to be the "Fly," schooner, of Whitby, with a crew of four hands, from Newcastle to London, with a cargo of bricks.

Lowestoft November 10th, 1861, A vessel was reported to have struck on the inner shoal, it was the "Undaunted," barque of Aberdeen, from Archangel to London, with oats. She was taken into tow by the Rainbow, but grounded near the North-pier. She was striking heavily at times, the swell being very considerable, coxswain Hook saved 11 crew. By the next day the "Undaunted," laid full of water on the North-beach; her stores had been safely landed.

On Thursday 5th December 1861, a meeting of the R.N.L.I was held at its house, John street, Adelphi, London; T. Chapman, Esq., in the chair. The Secretary read the minutes of the previous meeting. Rewards amounting to £28.10s. were voted to the crews of the Lowestoft and Pakefield Lifeboats, which are in connection with the National Lifeboat Institution, for putting off on the 10th and 14th November, and rescuing during heavy gales of wind, twenty- nine shipwrecked persons from the bark "Undaunted," of aberdeen, pilot cutter "Whim," and "Saucy-Lass," of Lowestoft. The Lowestoft steam tug redered important service to the Lifeboat in saving the crew of the pilot cutter and the lugger, and her crew of four men were paid £2 by the Institution. It was said that, owing to the dangerous position in which the cutter and lugger lay, during the gale on the sands, if the slightest accident of any kind had happened, or anything had given way, to either the Lifeboat or Steamer, the two-latter must to all appearance, have instantly gone to pieces. Captain Joachim., had gone off in the Lowestoft Lifeboat on each occasion, and the Institution voted to him his 3rd- service clasp, in admiration of his additional gallant services.

Wednesday 5th March 1862 a fatal wreck took place in the evening on the Corton Sand's, off Lowestoft. The brigantine "Matilda", of Stockholm, from Marseilles to Yarmouth, laden with oil cake, arrived off Lowestoft and then hoisted a signal for a pilot. The brig was boarded by a pilot from a yawl and stood on, when suddenly she struck heavily on the sands with the sea breaking over her. Three of the brig's crew and the Lowestoft pilot got away in her long boat and succeeded in reaching Lowestoft. Robert gathered a crew and the lifeboat was taken in tow by the harbour tug and proceeded to the wreck, and rescued three more crew along with the "Matilda's" captain. Two poor sailors, however, were drowned; and without the prompt arrival of the Lifeboat all who were left on board would have drowned, for a terrific sea was running that night, and the ship went to pieces within hours. Captain River's master of the harbour tug "Powerful" was awarded the thanks of the Institute on vellum for his part in the rescue.

On Saturday 10th May 1862, the schooner "Peri", Lewis, from Newcastle, of and for Salcombe, assisted of by Hook and the Old Company, and towed into harbour by tug, very leaky, and laid ashore. Agreement for services £70.

On Thursday 26th June 1862, the schooner "Agnes Fraser," Mackenzie, of Inverkerthing, from Gottenburg for London with oats and iron, grounded on the Newcome Sand, at about 1a.m., there took the assistance of the Old Company beachmen for agreement of £55, and was got off about 2.30a.m., making no water.

The anniversary of the Suffolk Humane Society and the Lowestoft Lifeboat Association was held on Wednesday 27th August 1862. The Society's Lowestoft and Pakefield boats were afloat in the harbour for the inspection of its subscribers and the public, and at 11.a.m. they were manned by their gallant crews, each proceeded to sea, having on board a number of ladies and gentlemen desirous of knowing something of the perils of the deep; but as Robert Hook, coxswain of the Lowestoft Lifeboat said," Although a stiff breeze was blowing from the south-east, "there wasn't sea enough to make any fun". At 2.p.m., the Manby apparatus for rescuing the crews of stranded vessels was exhibited on the south pier, the firing off of two rockets, also used to obtain communication with vessels, concluded the proceedings. The annual meeting was held at the Royal hotel, for the purpose of making awards, passing accounts, and electing a committee for the ensuing year. The following awards were made, the chairman, Major General Wingfield accompanying each by appropriate remarks to the receiver: To William Gilby, for having, on the 20th of June last, saved Frederick Woodrow, aged nine, who had fallen into the harbour, 5 shillings. Samuel Barnard, having, on the 5th June, saved the life of James Gallant, aged nine, who had fallen into the harbour, 5 shillings. Charles Day received 5 shillings for saving a child, named Balls, who had fallen off a raft in the harbour. Henry Norman 5 shillings, for saving on the 17th of August, a boy, aged ten years, who had fallen off old Billingsgate. William Neave 5 shillings, for saving Master Arthur Harvey, on the 11th of September 1861. Thomas Porter, James Boyce, Jar Peck, each received 5 shillings, for rescuing on the 30th November 1861, John Spurgeon and his son William, whos boat was so full of sprats that it sank with them, but not for their timely aid the father must have been drowned. Colin Whales, one of the band of the Lowestoft rifle volunteers, was awarded £1 for jumping off the pier steps by the reading rooms, and saving a young visitor, named Ellis, who had fallen into the water, the chairman remarked that he was doubly a volunteer. Samuel Butcher and Benjamin Butcher were awarded 10 shillings each- the former for saving Joseph Fletcher, and the latter James Mewse, whose boat had sunk from a squall off Kessingland on the 16th of April last. Robert Welham and John Heavers, two bridge-men, received 5 shilling each for saving a child named Byles, who on the 3rd August, who had fallen into the lock. James Nobbs was awarded £1 for saving, on the 16th December Last, a child, named Carr aged six, by jumping overboard into the harbour and rescuing him. Several other cases were adjourned, the parties not being present.

On the 13th January 1863, the brig "Mauney," Cook, of Arundel, from Portsmouth, for Sunderland, grounded on Holm-Sand at five a.m.; Took the assistance of Hook and the old beach company by agreement for £100, she was got off about noon and anchored in our North-roads making no water.

On Sunday 25th January 1863 in the recent heavy gales, the Lowestoft lifeboat rescued thirteen men belonging to the barque "Bonnie Dundee," of Dundee. For these and other services to shipwrecked crews the National Lifeboat Institution remitted to its Norfolk and Suffolk branch's £88.10s to pay the gallant men for their noble exertions.

On the 29th January 1863, the brig "Gosforth," Stebbing,

master, of and from Shields, for Southampton, with coal, grounded in the inner shoal, and took assistance from Hook and his fellow beach-men to get her off and into harbour, by agreement for £150. She was got off, and was left riding in the roads.

On the 20th May 1863, the Old Company assisted the brig "Alice Haviland," Robertson, of and from Shields, for London, with coals, for agreement of £60 in a leaky condition.

On Wednesday 19th August 1863 the Suffolk Humane Society and Lowestoft Lifeboat held their anniversary of this excellent institution, when the Society's boats were afloat for the inspection of subscribers and the public. Both boats took a trip seaward, numbers of visitors availing themselves of the opportunity to accompany the respective crews. At 3pm was held a demonstration of the mortar and rocket, for obtaining communication with stranded vessels, took place on the pier, when a lad was drawn across the mouth of the harbour, from the north to the south pier in the cradle, but not without being purposely immersed in the water beneath, to the no small amusement of the visitors. The annual meeting was held at 4pm at the Royal Hotel, General Wingfield occupying the chair. The following awards were made; Charles Benment, bridge-man, for saving the life of a lad who had fallen into the harbour,5 shilling's -Edward Drew, bridge-man, for saving the life of Richard Mann when going on board a fishing boat the light dazzled his eyes so that he fell into the water. Drew threw a rope where he heard the cry, it being too dark to see which Mann got hold of, and with the assistance of Captain Rivers, the harbour master, he was drawn out,10 shilling's -Samuel Chamberlin of the "Monarch" steam ship. A man fell into the water after striking himself in the dark against a crane. He twice threw a rope to him, and, with the help of the master of the "Industry" the man was saved, 10s- Joseph Hall, shipwright, for saving the life of James Miller, who was walking on a plank from a vessel to the quay, and fell into the harbour. Hall jumped in and got hold of the boy, and swam with him to the stage, £1- Robert. Hook, for saving the life of George Brown, who in the gale of the 21st December 1862,fell between his vessel and the pier,7s.6d- Thomas Colman for saving the life of a child named Thomas Webb, who had fallen into the water, and was being held by another child,2s.6d. William Palmer, a man of ill health, for saving William Hewitt, who had fallen into the water, another person holding palmers legs while he reached Hewitt,7s,6d.-Nathaniel Colby, coxswain of the Pakefield lifeboat, received the following sums for the days service, for crew,£1.15s;for getting the boat up and down,£1.15s;coxswain 5s;for lifeboat,£1.6s. Robert Hook, coxswain Lowestoft lifeboat, received £7.6s for also launching the boat. The Chairman complemented both coxswains on the efficient state of their boats.

 On the 9th September 1863, the Prussian brig "Adelhide," Captain Heinrich, of and for Stettin, for Havre, with timber, grounded on the Newcome-Sand about 3 a.m. Hook who was on look out, took out a yawl along with fellow old company men, she subsequently took the assistance of the beach-men, and was got off on the next tide, for a payment of £200.

On Tuesday 12th October 1863, the sloop "Peace," of Goole, was assisted off the Ness-Point into harbour by the old beach company, and towed into harbour for ballast; agreement, £30.

On Saturday 24th October 1863, the Sloop "Queen," Dyer, of Lowestoft, from Yarmouth, for Goole, with wheat, with pumps choked and the schooner "Prince Albert," Groves, of and for Yarmouth, from Rancorn, with salt, both grounded on the Holm-Sand at about six a.m. Both assisted off by the Old Beach Company, for £20 each.

On February 12th, 1864, the schooner "Schiedam", Fox, from London for Shields had beached in the storm the previous day. An agreement was made with Robert and the Old Company beach-men to get her off for £130.

CHILD BURNT TO DEATH. -On Saturday 13th February 1864, an inquest was held at Lowestoft before F.B.Marriott, Esq., Coroner, on the body of Benjamin Neeve, aged 4 years. From the evidence it appeared that the deceased had been left by his mother, and, being fond of playing with fire, had set his clothes on fire about five minutes after his mother was gone. An alarm was given by a neighbour who smelt the burning, and a fisherman named Robert Hook ran in and put out the fire by wrapping the child in his Guernsey shirt, which he had stripped off for the purpose. Dr.Matcham was sent for, and attended, and did all he could to save the poor little thing's life, but without success, for death put a period to his suffering soon after. - The jury returned a verdict of "Natural Death."

On Saturday 30th April 1864, the "Ann," of Guernsey, was run into while lying at anchor in our roads by the "Pilot," of Shoreham. The former sustained damage to the bowsprit, jib-boom, cutwater etc. She had to slip from her anchor, and proceeded for Shields, making water. The Old Beach Company received £40 in settlement for services rendered to her.

On Sunday 12th June 1864, the French brig "Chasemare-Don de Dieu," Patte, of Dunkirk, from Bowness for Calais, with pig iron, was assisted off the Holm-Sand by the Old Company beach-men, and into harbour at about 2p.m. The salvors were settled with for their services by Thomas Small, Esq., French-Vice-Consul, for the sum of £36.

On the Tuesday 9th August 1864 the marine fete came off on the broad waters of the roadstead. It was factionally remarked that the affair was "the pursuit of pleasure under difficulties," in so much as prior to the event and during it was drizzling rain and fast falling showers. It was said in the press that Napoleon, designated us English "a nation of shopkeepers"; we much question whether Aboukir and Trafalgar did not convince him that we were equally a nation of sailors, as we our more at home on the deep than behind a shop counter. The regatta this year had a prize pot of £110, there were eight races upon the card, but only seven were contested, there not being sufficient entries for the first, which was for a purse of 45 sovereigns, to be sailed for by yachts of 20 tons and upwards. The Second race was for a purse of 25 sovereigns for river yachts of 12 tons and upwards belonging to a recognized club. Four to start or no race. Half a minute per ton allowed for difference of tonnage. First boat to receive £20, second £5. For this prize the following entries were made: - Water Lilly, Red Rover, Isabella, Marguerate and Myth, the first three from Yarmouth and the last two from Norwich.

The "Isabella" did not sail, the course for these and other yachts and beach punts was in the form of a double triangle, measuring about six miles, the starting point being from the flag ship "Eliza" abreast of the south pier northwards, to a buoy off the nest point, then to the north Newcome buoy, then to the south-west boat, then to the north-west Newcome buoy round south flag boat off Pakefield to the starting point, twice round the course-12 miles. The following are the times recorded; -Red Rover 1hr,44m,37sec, Myth 1hr,46m,29 sec, Water Lilly,1hr,57m,12sec,Marguerate 1hr,57m,45sec, It was seen that the "Red Rover" had to allow her competitor "Myth" one minute due to rovers length the latter won then by twenty four seconds.

Skipping to the 3rd race for a total prize fund of 20 Sovereigns, for beach yawls from all parts. Four to start or no race. Half-a-minute per foot allowed for difference of length. First boat to receive £12; second £5; third £3. The entrance fee- First yawl 15 shillings-2nd 10s, and the third 5s towards the regatta fund. The course for the match was about 10 miles round, from the flag ship round the mark-buoys and boats then through the Pakefield gap and Stanford channel to the flag ship. This was sailed but only one round due to the lightness of wind and the unpleasantness of the weather. The contest between these noble boats was always much admired for the breadth of canvass carried, and the length and symmetry of their construction; nor were these the only features that caused the greatest interest, perhaps, but the fact that this class of boat is used by the gallant beach-men for rescuing life and property from the numerous sands that surround this coast. Only four boats entered the race, which are follows; -Violet, owner R.Roberts, Yarmouth, Eclipse, owner James Capps, Lowestoft, Thought, owner Henry Cook, Lowestoft, Bittern, owner Robert Hook, Lowestoft. The "Violet" did not take her place. At 13:16:45s the gun fired for the race to start, when up went a cloud of sail. "Bittern" taking the lead, followed by "Eclipse" and "Thought," but the wind being light, and the contest lying between Lowestoft boats, was watched with much interest. They came in as follows; Thought, Eclipse and last was Bittern.

The brig "Stockton-packet", Morley, of and from Middlesbrough, for Dunkirk, with pig iron; on the 28th Jan 1865. She had run onto the Holm Sand and was taking on water fast, Hook and the Old Company endeavoured to get her off and into harbour for repairs.

On Saturday 4th February 1865 the schooner "Armeias," Captain. Hubbard, of and from Hartlepool, for London, with coal, in going out of the Stanford Channel, at low water time, about noon, wind S.E., strong, with a heavy sea, struck in the channel, and the master hoisted a flag for assistance. Hook and his companions on seeing the flag of distress put off in their yawl to her aid, and succeeded in taking off the crew, when the schooner drove upon the Newcome sand, and sunk. The yawl was afterwards taken in tow by the harbour tug "Rainbow," and the crew were landed on the beach, and taken to the sailor's home, where they were cared for, and on the following day were sent home by W.Cole, Esq., the Honorary President of the shipwrecked mariner's society of Lowestoft.

On Monday 21st February 1865, the weather was most boisterous and pitiless that we have known here in Lowestoft for several years, thick snow storms from early morning followed each other in rapid succession throughout the day. During the stormy weather a large number of vessels had brought up in our North and South roads for shelter, but on the wind coming away from the West- South- West they were all on the move for their respective ports of destination, presenting one of those beautiful picturesque sights not uncommon with us. A number of casualties have been reported, the most serious of which is the loss of the French Chasemaree "Gilbert Alphonse," merchant, from Blyth, for Caen, with coals, which parted from her anchor about 10 p.m. of Monday, and came ashore off Corton. The coastguard-men at Corton used every exertion to save the crew, by throwing lines from a mortar over the vessel, but all in vain, owing to the raging of the storm, as they could not make the crew understand it's use, and it was not until seven a.m., of Tuesday that they were rescued from their perilous position by the Lowestoft Lifeboat and taken to the Warren-House, on Gunton- denes, where they received every attention their exhausted condition so much needed. They were subsequently removed to the sailor's- home.

On Monday 20th March 1865, the Danish schooner "Pfeil," of Blankenesse, from Hamburg for South America, grounded on the Newcome-Sands in the early hours of the morning. The crew were rescued by the Lowestoft Lifeboat, and taken into the port. In the course of the day the schooner was also got off the sands, and taken into Lowestoft.

On Thursday July 14th, 1865 was the day fixed by the Lowestoft Amusement Committee for the first of a series of marine fetes to be observed in the expanse of water in the Northroads. An excellent programme was advertised offering prizes to the amount of £60, to be competed for by yawls, beach gig, fishing luggers, rigged boats and mackerel tubs. The morning broke with a dull haze and a S.W.wind, which gradually increased to a No.6 breeze accompanied with heavy rain, and causing the waves to break over the south pier to the delight of onlookers.

The only race that took place was between six handsome and graceful yawls, for prizes totalling £20; the first boat to receive £12, the second £5, and the third £3. Half-a-minute per foot to be allowed for difference in length. First yawl to pay 15 shillings and the other five 10 shillings towards the regatta funds. The course was of an oval form, and about ten miles in length from the moorings opposite the pier sailing southerly, leaving all the buoys of the Newcome on the port side.

The following yawls where entered; Endurance, Southwold, Eclipse, owner, J.Capps, Thought, owner, H.Cook, Young Prince, owner, W.Newman, Bittern, owner, Robert Hook, and lastly Greyhound, owner, A.Allerton, all from Lowestoft.

An accident happened to the "Bittern" when proceeding out of harbour; owing to the strength of the wind, she fell across the bows of the steam tug "Rainbow" which was towing three other yawls, and was cut down to the water's edge and therefore prevented sailing. The only yawls that came to the mark were "Eclipse" "Greyhound" and "Thought" From the strength of wind the "Thought" was unable to get her moorings, but as soon as she got pretty close in line the signal gun when off for the start. Up when the three sails on each boat and away went the yawls,"Thought" gave up and returned to harbour, leaving the race to "Eclipse" and "Greyhound." The Former at one point was considered three miles ahead, but lost ground due to the strong winds and tide, leaving the "Eclipse" to take the 1st prize.

The schooner "Hannah-Booth", Prettyman, of Yarmouth, from Gottenbury, for Colchester, with deal and iron, got onto the Newcome Sand about 11 a.m. on the 31st July 1865, and was afterwards assisted off, making little water by Hook and the Old Company-agreement of £40.

On Tuesday 15th August 1865, it blew a gale from the South-West, when the "Light of the Harem," a brigantine, of Whitstable, from Hartlepool for Woolwich, with coals, was observed to be on Corton- Spit. Robert Hook launched the Lifeboat though heavy surf, and on proceeding to her they found she had two signals of distress flying, and that her bower anchor was let go. The crew were got out, and it was thought that if they unshackled the chain she might possibly come off. Several hands got on board and did so, and then left her and rode by in the Lifeboat. She afterwards came off, when hands were put back on-board, they made for Hewitts-gat, the Lifeboat hanging astern, when an agreement was made with the Yarmouth tug, "Pilot," for £15 to tow her to Lowestoft, where she arrived shortly after 5 p.m.

The schooner "Desire," M.Davies, of and from Portmadoc, for Forsdyke Bridge, with slate, anchored in the roads at one p.m. of Saturday 29th October 1865; at 10.30 a.m. next day, a derelict brig during the gale from S.S.W., caused her to part from her anchor when she drove into the "Desire." She was driven ashore dead opposite the Old Company shed, where she filled with water and sank. The crew where helped ashore by Robert Hook and the Lifeboat crew.

The Ipswich journal on Saturday 9th December 1865 reported on the adjudication of that of the brigantine "Grasshopper," John Batts, of Southhampton, from Hartlepool for Lymington, with coals, was assisted off the

North beach and into the harbour under agreement for £130. On Monday, the case was adjudicated at the court house, before Mr. Steward, Esq. (Chairman), and S.Waddington, Esq., the agreement being disputed.

Mr. Seago appeared for the salvors, Robert Hook, James Nenve and others, and Captain. Small for the owners and underwriters of the ship and cargo. The vessel was of the registered burthen of 104 tons, built in 1835, and the agreed value of £500, and her cargo £115, making a total of £615. It appears that the vessel was at anchor off Pakefield on Monday 27th of November 1865, when she had three feet of water in her and the master thought to take the harbour, and in attempting to do so, about 7pm, she missed and fell behind the north pier; the wind at the time blowing strong from the south west, and the tide ebb. She bent heavily on the ground and against the side of the pier. It was stated for the salvors, that it was impossible to board her from boats owing to the heavy range of sea at the back of the pier, and the only way of doing so was by jumping from the pier to the rigging as the vessel rolled in, and which was done at great risk to life and limb; that by means of a hawser ahead, which twice broke when heaved upon at the windlass (hoist) by some 18 or 20 men, and a spring rope from the starboard quarter to the pier, hauled at by some 50 or 60 men, she was gradually got a-head, and a larger hawser having been taken to the south pier in a boat which was nearly swamped in doing so, the vessel's head was ultimately turned into the harbour, when the jibs were set and she was taken into the harbour mouth and moored. They left at 10pm they say, the other side saying it was only 9pm. After getting into the harbour the salvors pumped, but declined to continue to do so after she was moored, they considering they had fulfilled their agreement. It was submitted that, but for the timely services of these men, their skill in the use of spring rope, she would in all probability have become a wreck.

James Neave, one of the beach-men, was sworn to the truth of the statement put in by Mr.Seago and Edward Elsegood coast-guardsman, and John. Gallehawke, chief boatman of that service, were examined in support, and both asserted that they would not have run the risk of boarding the vessel except for the purpose of saving life, and also that it was owing to the spring rope she did not go to the beach.

Mr.Small argued that the case was wanting in some of the principal ingredients of salvage. There was no great value of property saved; the vessel was thirty years old; the salvors brought no appliances at their own cost, no steamboat, warp, etc., the latter belonged to the vessel, and there was no length of service, the time not exceeding more than one-and-a-half hours.

He called and examined the Master, who did not materially contradict the foregoing statement, or bring out anything excepting that he let go his anchor when he found his vessel would not answer the helm; it however came home. Mr. Robert Massingham, the deputy harbour master, gave evidence principally as to the time elapsing from the vessel's getting ashore and her passing through the bridge, which he made to be an hour and a half. The court having been cleared, was shortly after reopened, when the chairman said the award in this case was that the salvors receive £85, the ship in addition paying the costs of hearing, £9.6s.0d.

On Friday 22nd December 1865, an adjudication was heard at the court at Lowestoft.- This was a claim for assistance rendered by Robert Hook and William Gallant and the Old Company of beach-men to the schooner "Ann Fleming", of Wick, Donald Campbell, master, from Thurso, with a cargo of paving stones, bound for Lowestoft, and which vessel, while at anchor off Lowestoft, was run into by the brig "Mary Jane", of London, Robert Stewart master, the former being dismasted, and the latter suffering loss of bowsprit etc. The salvors assisted in clearing away the wreck. The adjudicators were James Peto and Charles Steward. Mr Seago appeared for the salvors, and Captain Small for the owners and underwriters. The accidents took place on Friday 15th. Both vessels came into harbour. The court awarded the salvors £8, and costs £4.12s. The agreed value of ship and cargo was £650.

On Monday Jan 20th ,1866 an inquest was held at The Suffolk Hotel, before F.B. Marriot. Esq. The subject of which was the body of the pilot of the Austrian brig "Osip". Robert. Wm. Hook, Coxswain of the Lowestoft lifeboat, explained early in the morning of Saturday 13th at about 8am they saw a vessel on the East point of holm sand. A yawl called the "Young Prince" went out to her, and two of the crew got on board, but the Captain of the brig produced a revolver and threatened the two crew members of the yawl, so they withdrew. The Young Prince signalled for a larger one, which went off, and this yawl (Albatross) afterwards signalled for the lifeboat, which was launched and taken in tow by the steam tug "Rainbow" On arriving at the vessel the sea was breaking over her heavily, and there was so much "Ruffle"(spars and rigging) hanging over her sides, they could not get near. They dropped anchor, wore down, and after trying for some time, they were obliged to cut their cables to prevent being drifted on to the sands. They were taken into tow by the "Rainbow", got another anchor and cable, and were towed out a second time, and on arriving at the vessel she had become a complete wreck, her deck and topside being all gone. It was reported that Hook waded and swam through the surf reached the vessel and shouted out to the crew. At that point six members of the crew who he was trying to communicate with were hit with a strong wave, washing them over board where they headed for the lifeboat and were pulled aboard. Robert repeatedly threw a rope three times to the captain, but he refused to take hold and at that point a very heavy sea struck the pilot (deceased) and knocked him against the wreck, and cut his forehead. They managed to reach him with a boat hook and pull him into the boat, where his jaw was observed to move once, with seven crew members on board, they rubbed the deceased while coming ashore, and did what they could to restore animation. A report had got about that the pilot (deceased) had been given a kicking by the brigs crew for getting the

111

vessel aground. When asked by the chairman, Hook replied "I'm positive that I saw him standing on his feet with the crew before he was knocked overboard by the sea". He believed the pilot died from exhaustion and the blow, and nothing to do with the brigs crew. Richard Butcher Corroborated Hook's evidence. Robert Hook stated it was the worst sea he had experienced for nearly 20 years and without the help of the steam tug the lifeboat would have not reached the wreck. Verdict "Accidentally drowned".

The Osip of Fiume was bound from Falmouth, with a cargo of maize, for Hull, five of the crew of twelve where reported drowned which included its captain.

On Wednesday 31st January 1866, during the last tempestuous weather of our coast over the last week, the brig "Royal Union," of Sunderland, loaded with coals, for Calais, was lost on Corton-Sands, the master having mistaken his course in consequence of the removal of the light-ship, the master raised a flag of distress. Robert Hook on seeing the signal gathered his crew and launched the Lifeboat, on arriving at the vessel she started to break-up and he collected up the crew from the waves.

On March 22nd, 1866 Suffolk Humane Society and Lifeboat Association held a meeting at the court-house, to order the payment of certain bills, the amount of which being somewhat heavy. The committee did not want to incur the responsibility of discharging them without such a hearing. Charles steward, Esq., was called to the chair, amongst those present General Wingfield R A, Captain, Preston R. N.W Cole, G Seppings. Mr Preston informed the meeting that the Lifeboat had been off five or six times this year, and during these times three cables had been cut resulting in the loss of an anchor and the committee wanted to find out if it could have been prevented? One such case was that of the brig Osip, Robert. Hook was called to give account of his actions.

He was asked why he had cut the line on that occasion, He replied "We attempted to get near to the ship, dropped anchor but the risk to the boat and crew with the height of waves compelled me to cut the line"," My first responsibility is that of my crew, I would put them before the cost of an anchor". The bill for the new cables was £15, 9 shillings and altogether £70. The Chairman as in the case of the brig Osip, expressed his great admiration at the way in which the beach-men behaved in going to it, and spoke in high regard of Robert. Hook, Richard. Butcher, and the rest of the Lifeboat crew. After some further conversion, the bill was passed.

On April 7th, 1866, Robert Hook was called as a witness in the case of "Turgosso" v "Beal" and others, it was reported in the press at the time as follows.

This was a running down case in Lowestoft harbour on March 26th, 1866. Mr. O'Malley, QC, Mr. Keane, QC, and Mr. Stephenson for the plaintiff; Mr. Bulmer, QC, and Mr. Metcalfe for the defence. Mr. O'Malley stated the facts of the case to be addressed in support of the declaration.

Plaintiff, he said, was the owner of a sloop called, the "Odd Fellow", of Gainsborough, 39 tons burthen, and the defendants, John Beal, George Mabson and Robert Harding, were owners of a barque (sailing ship with the rear mast fore-and aft-rigged and the remaining two masts square rigged) of 311 tons, the "Abyssinian", of Whitby. The action was brought to recover damage for the injury that the plaintiff had sustained from the negligence, neglect, and want of skill and care in the navigation of the defendant's ship. On the afternoon of the 26th of March 1866, there blew a very high wind from the N.E, which was not, however such a gale as that a well-found ship would not be able to ride out. Somewhere about three or four o'clock the plaintiff's sloop entered the harbour of Lowestoft. There were two harbours properly so called at Lowestoft, one the inner or old harbour, which was for a considerable period the only harbour at Lowestoft; and there was another harbour, which was called the outer. The course of navigation for vessels generally was for all entering the outer harbour to go and pass through the narrow passage into the inner harbour, when they become subject to the regulation and direction of the harbour master. The tide at Lowestoft came down more or less strongly from the north, and on the day in question the wind was blowing from the N.E, so that the wind concurred in carrying a ship down to the south. The sloop Odd Fellow was out at the time of the gale coming on, and had got some distance away from Lowestoft towards the north, when the master received an injury to his hand. He is having the wind directly in his teeth, as a prudent act, made for Lowestoft.

The course of a ship coming from the north, which was about to make for the harbour, should be always to have the sail set aft, and as the ship came in through the piers to luff up the wind, and there cast anchor, or not as the occasion might require. When the plaintiff's sloop came into the outer harbour, the master found it was very full of vessels; it was so full that the direct course from the entrance into the inner harbour was entirely blocked up by vessels that were waiting their turn to get into the harbour. It was therefore, of the utmost importance to him, as soon as he had luffed up into the wind and to avoid collision to drop his anchor. The ground at that place was rather uneven, and the anchor consequently dragged till the sloop was brought up by the south pier-a place quite safe enough for a small vessel like the defendants. Shortly after the sloop was lying in its position, completely out of reach of any vessel that might get in and out of the way of collision, defendants banque, which was also coming down from the south, made for Lowestoft harbour. They had no right whatever to attempt the harbour at that time, and could have ridden out the gale in the roadstead, or could have gone before the wind to Harwich, there being no room in the harbour for such a vessel, and an entrance only being possible without damage of some sort or other. The banque was in ballast, and high above the water, and he should show by evidence that she was not signaling to enter. At that time, it would be shown that there was no aft sail on the banque. The result of the banque's entering the harbour was a collision between her and the sloop Odd Fellows, whereby the latter was sunk and was lost, together with the cargo of chalk. As he understood if the master of the banque had expressed his willingness to re-numerate the plaintiff for the damages; but the Mutual Assurance Society, at Whitby, to which he belonged, had objected, and determined to defend this action. The following witnesses were called on behalf of the plaintiff: -Alfred. Wilburn, Master of the sloop, who described the circumstances as briefly given in the learned counsel's address; Thomas. George. Hughes, ship owner, Robert. Hook, Richard. Butcher & William. Jeckell, owners of fishing smacks, who all agreed generally in the statement that the banque was managed in an un-seaman like manner.

The Jury retired to consider, and after a few minutes returned a verdict for the plaintiff damages £350, the court rose soon after 3pm.

On the 31st July 1866, the schooner "Alfred", Cockerall, of Colchester, from Shields, for Maldon, with coal. Assisted off Corton Sand, Leaky, and into Harbour by Robert and the Old Company, about 10p.m.

On the 3rd August 1866, the brig "Wave", Towell, of Stockton, from Wybury for Weymouth, with deal, helped into Harbour by the Old Company, while filled with water, Leaky.

On Saturday 1st September 1866, the barque "J. S. Schwen, Sen", Voight, from Kragero, for London, with wood and ice; got upon the Holm-Sand early in the morning, although having a local pilot on board. She was assisted off by the Old

Company and anchored in the North-Roads at about one p.m., the same day, making no water. Agreement was for £200. The vessel proceeded on the following Monday for London as there was no damage.

Salvage Services: - The cases of the schooner "Daniel", and the sloop "Eva", which were assisted from the rear of the North pier by the beach-men of the Old Company, paid by Mr. Bradbeer, the former for £85, and the latter for £47.10s.

During the week starting from the 30th November 1866, proved to be busy for Robert and his fellow-beach-men of the Old Company. The weather during this week had been change-able with strong winds from South-West, and rain; the drum had been hoisted several times. (Crews would hoist a drum to indicate assistance required) On the 30th the schooner,"Stour," Butler, of Harwich, from London, for Newcastle, with pine-deal, in getting under way, missed stays and came to the beach opposite the Royal Hotel. On the tide falling her crew walked ashore. She was since got off and into harbour by the beach-men of the Old Company, agreement of £75, and the following day Wednesday was taken in tow by the "Robert Owen," and proceeded for Harwich. The smack Atalanta, of Lowestoft, belonging to Messrs.Rouse and Powell, while towing with other vessels to sea, the tow rope broke, and she came to the South beach near the wreck of the "Happy Family," where she filled with water, and was abandoned by her crew and soon after became a total wreck, so calm were the waters on that day in what is known as "Abraham's Bosom," little or nothing was saved from her.

The past week had been one of a succession of storms and rain accompanied with many casualties and loss of property and life. - On Wednesday 12th December 1866, the fishing lugger "William and Mary," of Yarmouth, got on the Barnard Sand at about 5 a.m., and became a wreck. On seeing the wreck, the Lifeboat made haste, Hook picked up two hands, with a Kessingland yawl saving one and the Pakefield Lifeboat the other, and the rest (seven or eight hands) were drowned. By this case and others, it was seen that the Barnard Sand was causing havoc. Robert Hook, Coxswain informed that the sand was getting much worse than formerly, as a short time since it would not "pick up," a fishing lugger, as in the past there was sufficient water for her to sail over it.

On Saturday 5th January 1867, the wind was strong from about the South-West, when the schooner "Reaper," Bundy, of and from Southampton, for Stirling, with bark, was assisted off a Lee-shore opposite the esplanade by Robert Hook and the old company beach-men, and into harbour by tug. The services have been settled for by Mr.B.M.Bradbeer at £54, and tug there out received £8.

At about three p.m. on Wednesday the 16th of January 1867, the salvors Robert Hook and Richard Butcher and others, of the Old Company, were on Lowestoft pier, when they saw the schooner "Ellen" riding abreast of the Wellington Esplanade, the wind at the time blowing a hurricane from the N.E with a tremendous sea running. Very shortly after, the schooner "Victory", of Ipswich, parted from her anchor causing her to ram into the "Ellen", carrying away the Ellens bowsprit and figure head. The Ellen then hoisted a flag of distress in her main rigging, but so fearful was the gale that no boat, other than a Lifeboat, could possibly render assistance, and since there were a number of vessels in the harbour requiring assistance, meant that coxswain Hook could not find a sufficient number of men to launch the Lifeboat as no men could be mustered. The salvors remained on watch all night, and at about 5 a.m. of the following day, the weather having somewhat moderated, though still blowing a gale from N.E. and the air was thick with snow, they manned their large course weather yawl with 16 hands, and pulled out of Lowestoft Harbour through a heavy sea to the Ellen. On approaching her they let go their anchors and veered down to her. They observed that she still had her signal in the main rigging, a waif at the main topmast head, and that she was riding with both anchors down. At great risk Robert and six other men jumped on board, and found but two hands on board, the rest of her crew having got on board the Victory on the previous day. Robert found the Ellen damaged and making water, and on his asking the master if he required assistance, he replied "YES PLEASE", and at once gave up charge of his vessel to him. The salvors attended the pumps, cleared the rigging away, and having made agreement with the tug Rainbow, they with much difficulty slipped the anchors, and the Ellen was towed into Lowestoft Harbour, and their safety moored. The Old Company was awarded £50 for the service. Some days later some children playing in the surf on the North beach, discovered the Ellen's decapitated figure head, but due to the vessel having left

Lowestoft she found a new home on the trophy wall of the Old Company shed.

On March 18th, 1867 there was an Adjudication, the brig Grace, Longstaff, of Sunderland. The claims of Robert Hook and others of our Old Beach Company, for services rendered to the above brig, in laying out an anchor and therefore rescuing the crew, on the night of the 6th inst, were adjudicated at the court house on Monday last, by R.C.Fower and Edward Leathes, Esq. Mr Seago appeared for the beach-man, and Mr. Archer for the owners of the brig. It appeared that the vessel was assisted from Great Yarmouth by Yarmouth beach-men, and in being towed into Lowestoft harbour, about 5pm, struck the south pier and was taken by the tide to the back of it where she came to the ground. Robert. Hook and his men manned their coarse weather boat Faith, and proceeded out of the harbour to the brig and offered their services, which at first where refused by the brigs captain, and within 10 minutes he changed his mind and accepted Hooks offer, and an anchor was laid in an E.S.E direction. They then commenced heaving, and also pumping, as the brig was taking on water. At 10pm they had managed to bring the vessels bow around to a south-south-east direction, they under the direction of the master, J. D.Wardropper, slacked the chain, which allowed her to drive further up the beach, they are intending the next morning to have cleared her of water, and lightening her of part of her cargo they then hoped to get her off. The master and crew where then landed about 10.15pm. Robert Hook and John

Gullihawk, chief coastguard boatman at the port were examined in support, and Mr. W. T. Balls, auctioneer, who had been sent for, stated that he had that day sold the hull and stores of the vessel for £1707.-Mr Archer in his address, stated that the salvors had been employed because they had said they could get the vessel off. The vessel was of considerable value, and it was entirely through the negligence of those employed she had been lost. Where services were rendered they should be paid for, but in this case the vessel and cargo had been lost, and the master and crew thrown out of employment, because of their own negligence. The Chairman (Mr. Fowler) in announcing the decision of the court that they were surprised the matter had been brought before them, it being a case that ought to have been settled out of court. The beach-men had endeavoured to render what service they could, and though the vessel was now a total wreck, their intention had been good, and the court awarded them £20, the costs, £5,6s also to be paid by the ship.

On Saturday 22nd March 1867, the brig "Quay-Side," Brown, of Whitby, from London for Hartlepool, having got upon the Ness-point, was assisted off by the Old Beach Company and into harbour by tug. Agreement, £100 of which the tug received £10.

On Friday 23rd May 1867, during a strong breeze a brig was observed to take ground on the bar of the Stanford Channel. The Lowestoft and Pakefield Lifeboat of the National Lifeboat Institution were there-upon launched and proceeded to the spot. The Pakefield boat took four men off the tail-rail (a rail around a ships stern) of the vessel, and at this point a wave pushed the brig completely over on its side. Robert Hook skillfully placed the Lowestoft boat between the masts so that the remaining eight hands dropped off the fore and main rigging into her. The brig was the "Amicizia," of Genoa, bound from Newcastle to Savona with a cargo of anchors, chains, and coals. She became a total wreck.

Suffolk Humane Society: - A meeting of the committee was held at the Court-House, on Wednesday 5th June 1867, James. Peto, Esq., occupying the chair. There were also present Captain. Preston, R.N., W. Jecks, Esq., G. Seppings, Esq., F.Morse, Esq., R.H. Reeve, Esq., W.Cole, Esq. Mr Preston, who kindly undertakes the supervision of the Lifeboats, reported that the Lowestoft boat, when hauled up, was found very defective, owing to the fore and aft tanks leaking, and several of the timbers amid-ship having been injured. The former was owing he thought, to marine glue having been used in the construction of the tanks, which were wood, covered with no.1 canvass, painted with three coats of paint. The wood had, from the wet, swollen, and the canvass, from the same cause, had shrunk, and thus wide openings had been found which admitted water. The injury to the timbers, he was of the opinion, had arisen from the form of the keel, which was of iron and convex, so that the weight of the boat, if she thumped the ground, or when standing in the boat-house, would rest on the centre of the keel, and forcing the timbers upwards, would product

"Hogback." The Lowestoft boat had been repaired at an expense of some £38, and the Pakefield boat, now requiring to be attended to, would render the present an expensive year, as the cost of both would go into the current year's accounts. Their usual plan was to repair in alternate years, so as to equalize expenditure. An order was made for carrying out the necessary repairs by Mr S.Sparham, under the superintendence of Mr. Preston. - Mr. Preston also stated that he had received a letter from Richard. Lewis. Esq., Secretary to the R.N.L.I., complaining that in the case of the Genoese brig "Amicizia," the Pakefield and Lowestoft boat both went off to the rescue, thereby increasing the expense, when it was presumed the windward boat would have been sufficient, and requested that the attention of the coxswains should be called to such an unprecedented case. Hook was asked on his opinion on why both boats were launched, and he gave the following response: "The two stations are barely in sight of each other in clear weather, and in gales, when vessels are in distress, were one boat to wait to see if the other had launched, many lives might be lost." but at the same time, the committee believe that if one boat were seen afloat or launching, with a prospect of performing the duty in question, the other would immediately desist. The meeting then separated.

Lowestoft, September 30th 1867: - The brig "Ameliora", Armstrong, of and for Blyth, from London (ballast), grounded on Newcome about 2.30p.m. On Sunday, and was assisted of about 6.30p.m., by the Old Beach Company, making no water. Agreement £20. She afterwards anchored in the roads, and proceeded next morning.

The "Kesiah Page", wilcox, of and for Folkestone, from Blyth with coal, struck on the Holm at 3 p.m., on the 23rd October 1867, was assisted off at 8 p.m., on the flood tide, by the Old Beach Company (agreement of £150), and was then anchored in Lowestoft roads, making no water.

From Monday 7th to Sunday 17th November 1867, gales from the E.N.E., raged along the Norfolk and Suffolk coast. Six vessels were driven ashore between Lowestoft and Kessingland, most of which were total wrecks. A fine barque is also ashore to the North of the harbour. A large barque and a Yarmouth schooner were sunk at sea, three of the crew of the latter being drowned. The schooner "Medora," Greystone, of and for Yarmouth with coal, drove upon the Newcome Sands, the lifeboat reached the unfortunate vessel, and found two men in the rigging. These were got off in an exhausted condition and landed at the sailor's home. The master, his son, and his boy made an attempt to gain the shore in their boat, but shortly after they left the vessel, the boat was capsized by a tremendous sea with all three drowned.

On the 25th July 1868, the French brig "Leopold Augusta", Bossence, from Peterborough, for fecamp, with wheat, having grounded on the Newcome Sand, was assisted off by beach-men of the Old Company, and into harbour by the tug "Rainbow". The services have since been settled for by

Thomas Small, Esq., French Vice-Consul, for £130.

 On August 1st, 1868 started the Lowestoft Marine Fete within eye range of the pier, programmed by the Amusement Committee for the present season took place and consisted of sailing, rowing, paddling and swimming matches. The weather was hot and bright but due to a lack of wind the sailing matches where delayed for later in the day. The pier with its approaches was decked out in bunting, while shoals of spectators packed the pier, esplanade, and every available vantage point along the sea front.

 The Second Boat race of the day was between six oared gigs, manned as they pleased. First boat to receive £3.10s, Second £1.10s and the 3rd ten shillings. Course was from the flag ship to the ness point north and back. The following contested these prizes, and caused much excitement. I'll try, owner Wm.Norman (Lowestoft), Sailors Friend, owner Chas. Liffen (Lowestoft), Fear not , owner Wm. Palmer (Lowestoft), Jenny Lind ,owner Robert Hook (Lowestoft), Quebec, owner John Adams (Lowestoft) and lastly the Alexandra, owner H Lawrence (Southwold). The latter boat entered after time and was objected to as being a river boat. They Came in as follows: -Jenny Lind, I'll Try, Quebec and sailor's friend, another win for Bob Hook and his Lifeboat crew.

 During the past week the wind continued to prevail from the S.W., with occasional rains. Sunday was almost a complete day of heavy rain, quite in contrast with the same time the previous year, when you had the novel pleasure of walking over the top of the " Walking -Gate," at the south-west corner of Arnolds field, leading into Raglan-Street, upon crisp snow. Owing to the mildness of the season, vegetation is very early, even summer flowers were in blossom. The fishing smack "Nautilus," of Lowestoft, owned by Captain. Coombes, when coming in from sea, about 7.30 p.m of the 17th January 1869, was reported to have grounded on the Holm-sand and sank, having on board about eighty packages of fish. Once the Lifeboat arrived to pick up the crew of four, they were more interested in saving their catch than their own lives. Some of her catch was saved by the beach-men, but she was fully insured.

On Friday Jan 29th, 1869 at 2am the Beach-men were aroused by the coast-guard-men on duty, who informed them that a ship was burning flares on Corton watch, known by the beach-men as Rattling Tom, wind blowing hard from S.W by S, thick with rain, they made their way to the North Road Company Boat-shed, but as they could see nothing they returned home at about 4am. They were again awoken by two men from Corton, who told them that their yawl had been off, but was obliged to put back without being able to rescue the crew of the vessel in distress, they said you can see the vessel from Corton as it was showing a light. The brave beach-men at once launched their Lifeboat, and accompanied by Mr. John Henderson, chief officer of the coastguard proceeded towards the spot indicated, but it took some-time to find the vessel, as the sea was breaking hard around the vessel. After discovering her they dropped their anchor to windward, and endeavoured to bear down to her, but owing to the tide and heavy sea they could not get to her, and could do nothing but pull anchor and stand down seeing which, the unhappy crew of which turned out to be a brig, fearing the Lifeboat was going to leave then cried out to the Lifeboat crew. The Lifeboat having tacked, succeeded in gaining the vessel, which was now laying on her broadside with her topsail in the water, the brigs crew which totaled eight in number were then taken off into the Lifeboat. Just at that point an accident occurred, which might have proved fatal to Robert Hook; the gallant coxswain of the Lifeboat. Just as the last man got into the Lifeboat the top mast of the brig came down and knocked Hook over board, he was able to seize hold of the main rope and was gladly hauled on board. The Lifeboat was then taken in tow back to Lowestoft by the steam tug "Rainbow", once landed the crew from the brig where taken into the sailor's home for a dry set of cloths and a hot meal. The brig turned out to be the "Queen of the Tyne", of shield, bound for London and carrying a cargo of coal.

In addition to the proceeding after Judgement, a solemn instance of the uncertainty of life occurred at the court house, when William Gallant, a member of the lifeboat crew and beach-man, about 44 years of age, who had been listening to the case, suddenly expired. Mr. May having certified to the coroner that the deceased had been suffering from a diseased heart, the formality of an inquest was not deemed necessary. He left a wife and several children. He would later be remembered in 1892 for his part of the rescue of the "Osip."

On Monday 1st of February 1869 the North-road Company observed a fore and aft schooner was lying on Corton-spit, wind at the time blowing hard from the S.W to S. The beach-men were at once called together, and the Lifeboat launched, and sail made for the vessel, and on coming along side found nobody was onboard. Hook boarded the schooner and found a fine retriever dog with brass collar on board and a cat, were these left to perish questioned Hook he said at a later date, so putting one under each arm drove into the water and passed them into the boat. The Lifeboat was towed back into harbour by the steam tug, but before getting to shore the schooner had gone under water. Her name was "Horace A. Bell, but lettered on the stern "St Andrew's N.B" she was from Fecamp bound to Yarmouth with a cargo of barley. The dog was returned to her master and the cat made a great addition to the Old Company Boat shed.

On Friday 12th of February 1869 it was reported, that during a heavy north-easterly gale, the Laetitia Lifeboat of the National Lifeboat Institution, was launched to the assistance of several vessels that were exhibiting signals of distress in the roads, near Corton- Gatway. The brig "Beatrix," from Hartlepool for London, with coals, was discovered with her mainmast cut away. At the request of the master the lifeboat remained alongside, and ultimately, with the assistance of a steam tug, Hook and his crew safely got the vessel and crew into Lowestoft harbour.

On the night of the 16th February 1869, Robert Hook and the Lifeboat crew attended the Town hall for the event of Adam's Lifeboat Fund. A night of entertainment, consisting of vocal and Instrumental music, Interspersed with readings, in aid of the above fund. Mr. Adam's had laboured so perseveringly in his benevolent efforts, he was rewarded with an overflowing house.

On Saturday 6th March 1869 the Norfolk Chronicle reported on the Gales on Wednesday last. The brigantine "Amelia" of and from Torquay for Hartlepool, with a cargo of ballast, when riding in Corton roads at 5 a.m., on Wednesday, commenced driving, winds strong from the north. A second anchor was let go, and the jib and foretopmast stay sail were hoisted to pay the ship off, but before the anchor took hold she struck heavily on Holm sand, and soon filled with water. The crew took to the boat, which was found much damaged, but succeeded in getting the crew on board the "Anna Louisa," of Rye, from whence Robert Hook and crew took them into the lifeboat and landed them in Lowestoft by 8am. The vessel soon after totally disappeared, "Amelia's" crew were received at the Sailor's Home, and have been sent home by Mr W.R.Cole, the honourable agent of the shipwrecked mariner's society at Lowestoft.

On Thursday 16th of March 1869 an adjudication took place at the Court House, Mr. Chamberlain proceeded to open the plaintiff's case, and said the case is as follows. The collision in question took place in Lowestoft's South roads, on Tuesday 9th of February, between three and four o'clock in the afternoon, and the fact was that both vessels were heading south. The wind was N.N.W by N, and it was such a wind that the vessels could not keep their course through Lowestoft-Roads, and they were obliged to bear. The Sarnia was close hauled on the starboard tack, and the Queen was on the port tack. That being the state of things, the Queen, instead of bearing up, as she was bound to do, kept her reach, and reached completely into course of the schooner. He didn't hesitate to say that the Sarnia ran into the Queen on the starboard quarter, close to the stern; but the old rule was for vessels on the starboard tack to keep their reach, and those on the port tack to bear up.

There would be no difficulty in regard to the question of damages, the parties in this action having already agreed upon this part of the case. Mr. Chamberlain then called Robert Hook, who said:" I am a beach-man, and master and owner of a vessel at Lowestoft"." I have been used to the sea 30 years". "I remember Tuesday the 9th of February, in the afternoon of that day I was on the South Beach, about 150 yards from the sea". "The wind was West by North, and it was just slack tide". "I observed the Sarnia and the Queen come into collision about a quarter of a mile off shore". "At the time of collision both vessels were under sail". "The Sarnia was heading nearly S.W. with perhaps a little on either side". "She was on the starboard tack, and the Queen on the port tack, both vessels were close hauled". "The Queen's head was about N.N.W". "There was a nice fresh breeze, and these vessels were the northern most part of the fleet".

Joseph Ellis, one of the old Company, at Lowestoft agreed with the evidence given by Hook. He added that in his opinion there was nothing to prevent the Queen bearing up and avoiding the Sarnia.

On Monday 30th august 1869 it was the annual Lowestoft Regatta in the road-stead, and was witnessed by a vast gathering of spectators. The bright and sultry weather of the previous weeks gave way on the Sunday to clouds and strong winds, but on Monday it was sunny with a mild wind. The Committee, sided by their secretary, Mr. W.G Chambers, had drawn up an excellent programme, but with the fresh North-North-East wind only a limited program was carried out. The first race of the day was between beach yawls, from Lowestoft, for a purse of £20; a quarter of a minute allowed per foot for difference in length. First boat to receive £12; second £5; third £3. The course was that of the double triangle, as usually adopted, having its base from the inner shoal buoy on the north, to the flag-boat moored off Pakefield on the South.

The sailing matches started South with a spanking breeze from the N.N.E. The following were the entries: - Happy New Year, Owner Robert Hook, Bittern, Owner James Ayers, Success, owner John Mewes. The race started at 12.24., Bittern taking the lead, but which Happy New Year did not long allow her to retain. They presented a good sight at starting, and afterwards as each yawl tore through the waves as the strong breeze allow them too, showing the visitors to the town how they would laugh at dangers when flying to the rescue of imperiled life and property. They went one round and finished as follows: - Happy New Year, BItttern and Success.

The Second race was for the prize of the value of £25, for cutter yachts and schooners, not exceeding 25 tons belonging to a recognized Yacht club. First prize a plate and £15, second £10. Schooners to be allowed at the rate of two-thirds tonnage. Time, half a minute per ton. Entrance fee 10s.6d. The following appeared on the cards as competitors:- Red Rover, owner S.Nightingale., Port Yarmouth, Waveney Queen, Owner Col Leathes, Port Lowestoft, Florence Nightingale, owner E.H.Everard, Port Yarmouth, Ariel, Owner T.read, Port Yarmouth, Otter, owner R .Pratt, Port Lowestoft, Cygnet, Owner H.Bullard, Port Yarmouth. This match was looked forward to with much interest, but lost much of its attraction from the fact only Red River, Waveney Queen, and Otter started; and also, the fact Waveney Queen fell out shortly after starting the race. The yachts came in as follows; - Red Rover and Otter second, The Waveney Queen was towed in by the Rainbow.

The Third match, for prizes value £15, between half decked local River Cutters and Latteen Yachts, under 12 tons. First yacht to receive a plate to the value of 12 sovereign's, 2nd prize £5. Winning yacht to pay £1.1s, and 2nd 7s.6d to the Regatta Fund. Here again disappointment as only three of the carded six yachts started the race. Only Marguarits, Sand, and Haleyon braved the stormy winds that blew, and they staggered and dipped, it made the spectators nervous as they looked at them, while the experienced eye of the yachtsmen could see the crafts had got all they needed to race. The yachts came in as follows: - Sand, Marguarits and Haleyon.

The Final Race was for a prize of £7.10s, between Six oared Beach Gigs, First to received £5; 2nd,£2; 3rd 10 shillings. The entries were all Lowestoft Gigs, as follows: - Jenny Lind, Owner Robert Hook, Sailors Friend, Owner James Ayers and Mosquito, Owner John Mewes. The start was good, as was the whole race and well contested with them coming in as the same order as above. The two latter matches caused much merriment, later that night at 9pm the event was finished off with a good display of fireworks in the harbour.

On Saturday 18th December 1869, the lifeboat Laetitia, of the National Lifeboat Institution, has been the means of saving the crew of eight men of the "Adina" of London, cargo of coal and arsenic, which was wrecked on the Holm Sands on Tuesday morning. During a heavy gale on the previous evening, a Dutch vessel the "St -Antonrus", in making for the harbour, struck the north pier, and afterwards became a total wreck. A further schooner was also wrecked on the Monday night on Corton Sands; the crew both saved by the Lowestoft Lifeboat.

On the 28th of December 1869, the schooner "Queen-of-the-Chase", William, of Blyth, from St-Michael's, for Hull, with oranges; grounded on the Newcome Sand and got off by the Old Company, agreement £65 plus one case of Oranges;

Towed into harbour by tug, having lost several sails.

On Friday 31st December 1869 the papers reported on Hook's Christmas Day rescue. The Laetitia Lifeboat, of the National Lifeboat Institution, was launched about one o'clock on Christmas morning to the assistance of a vessel which had gone on the Holm Sand. The Lifeboat was towed to the vessel by the "Rainbow" steam-tug, and was happily successful in bring safely ashore the master and crew of nine men from the wreck, which proved to be that of the three masts North German schooner "Agathe Scheilbert" of and from Stettin for Bordeaux, with timber. For many years after the name board from this schooner decorated the front of the old company's boathouse.

On the same day as the above schooner, the three-mast schooner "Cornucopia", Storm, of Inverness, from Shields, for Lisbon, with coals, struck on Corton Sands, the schooner beat herself off, and was afterwards run into the beach at the ness-point, the crew being rescued by the Lifeboat crew and Old Company as they returned to the Old Company shed from the above rescue. On Boxing Day her cargo of coals was being thrown out to lighten her, hoping to get her off on the next high tide. This ill-luck to the schooner provided the poor an opportunity of replenishing their coal heaps gratuitously, and which the sharpness of the weather prompts them actively to take advantage of.

On Thursday 25th May 1870, the brigantine, "Dido", Collings, of Little Hampton, from Shields, with a general cargo for

Ambriz, on the Africa coast, beating in through the roads while in the afternoon she struck the ground upon the Newcome Sand, the outer buoys having been mistaken for the inner buoys, owing to the colour having been recently changed. Robert and fellow company members came to an agreement for the sum of £100 to get the vessel off and into safety, and in the afternoon, they succeeded in floating and anchoring her in the roads, and as she had no damage she proceeded off on her voyage.

On Tuesday 29th June 1870, the lifeboats at Corton and Lowestoft, in connection with the Royal National Lifeboat Institution, were afloat for their usual quarterly exercise; and although there was not so much wind as could have been desired to test the merits of the boats, those on board had a very pleasant trip. After being under canvas some time, the sails were furled, and oars shipped, and a most exciting race between the two boats ensued. The Corton boat was under the charge of W. Jecks, Esq., Local Honorary Secretary; the Lowestoft boat under Mr. Henderson, chief officer of the Coastguard. There were also present General Windfield, R.A., Colonel Leathes, J.J. Colman, Esq., j. Lee. Barber, Esq., F. Ranson, Esq., and other gentlemen.

The regatta season of 1870 was remembered as one in which Lowestoft, with reference to its marine regattas, was as Robert described "Lying upon its oars". This was down to the low wind and flat sea, but it was recorded that Kirkley and Pakefield had made a united effort, under the leadership of W.Warman. Esq., ably seconded by Mr. James.

Mickleborough and other gentlemen, to provide a regatta for the amusement of visitors, and that prizes amounting to 50 Guineas, had been offered for competition by yachts, yawls, gigs, punts, etc. (one guinea= 21 shillings £1.05) in old money. On Thursday 25th August, the regatta came off in the Lowestoft roadstead, running parallel with the bold cliffs of these twin sister towns- one side of the old street Kirkley and the other side Pakefield. The morning started with fair weather, but soon afterwards it became cloudy, heavy rains falling causing many an anxious look windward. A heavy down-pour fell during the afternoon, but didn't last too long. The committee's tent was pitched upon the cliff opposite the south end of the new terrace, where was reared a very capital stand, but which was not thickly tenanted, the esplanade, the cliff, and beach affording so good a view of the proceedings, and which got more crowded as the afternoon wore on. The Southwold pilot cutter, was dressed in bunting, and acted as flagship. There were eight matches announced, the first of which was to be sailed by yachts under 30 ton's. Otter came in first for a prize of 5 guineas and a silver cup. The second match was between yawls and it was between 3 boats, and came in as follows; - Sophia, Reliance and Happy Returns last. The most exciting match was between six-oared beach-gigs for a purse of six guineas, 1st prize 3guineas, 2nd prize 2guineas. And 3rd prize 1guinea. The entries were as follows; - Naiad, Fisher, pakefield; Jenny Lind, Hook, Lowestoft; Alexandra, Woods, Lowestoft; Try, Laws, Southwold. Before the race Naiad was withdrawn. A good start was affected from the beach, but soon after the "Try" was seen to make for the shore with a broken oar. On landing, the crew entered a protest against the "Jenny Lind" for fouling them and driving them against the flagship. The "Jenny Lind" took the lead and kept it. One round should have decided the match, but the gun not having been fired on passing the flagship, both boats went a second round, which was a sad waste of strength. The whole affair closed with an excellent display of fireworks from opposite the new terrace.

The smack "Olive," T.Calver master, from Grimsby when going out of Corton Gat on Wednesday 12th October 1870, about noon, struck upon a wreck close to the third buoy out, and afterwards upon the patch. The anchor was let go, but came home, and the vessel drove upon the sand. The smacks little rowing boat was ready to get out, but the sea broke on board and stove her, and after they got her out, she came into the smack and sank. Signals of distress were burnt. The Corton Lifeboat men saw them, and could have reached them an hour before she did, but being fishing time, had not sufficient hands to launch her; she brought away, and the Lowestoft Lifeboat, which got to the wreck about the same time, took off the remaining twelve hands. They were brought to the sailors home about 8.30 a.m., well taken care of, and on Thursday were forwarded to Harwich by W.Cole, Esq. The master lost part of his thumb.

On the sand on Wednesday 7th December 1870,- the "Dazzler", Fryer, of and from Whitstable, for Shields, just in ballast, owing to having to pass under a brig's stern early on

Wednesday, being unable to put about after she had been stayed, came to ground on the North part of the Newcome-Sand, where she remained ten minutes, then hoisted a signal for a tug, but in the two hours she was waiting for a tug she filled with 8.1/2 feet of water in her hold. Robert and five others, took a small gig the "Jenny Lind" over to the vessel and the six beach-men were engaged to pump, under agreement for £36; the agreement for the harbour tug was for £50. In the course of the afternoon the "Dazzler" was towed into the inner harbour and laid on the mud.

On Wednesday 14th December 1870 a barque, "Forest flower" of Scarborough, from America for Newcastle, loaded with lead, during a thick fog at 8am struck the Holm sand. If that wasn't bad luck enough as she struck the sand, she ploughs into the remains of the Glenora lost at that exact spot on 18-10-1870.She immediately started to take on water. At daylight she was observed by the beach-men, who launched the Lifeboat and her brave crew, under the gallant coxswain, Robert Hook, proceeded off, followed by the steam tug rainbow, and the lifeboat crew succeeded in getting the crew of 16 hands, then the rainbow towed the Lifeboat to harbour. The weather remained strong but some of her stores where salved until the water level reached 8 feet within the vessel and she was left to mother nature to finish off her work.

At about 9 p.m., on Monday night of the 21st January 1871, the brig "Lizzie-Ann," Rutherford master, of and from Sunderland for Alexandria, with coal, got on the North-end of

Corton-sand, and sank. Bob Hook launched the Lifeboat but between the time it took to launch and get to the "Lizzie-Ann," the master and crew, consisting of seven hands, had took to their own boat. Jeremiah Helian, an able seaman, was drowned from this brig. The crew were taken to the sailor's home. Two days later on the Wednesday around 9 a.m., the sloop "John and Susannah," of Lowestoft, left port laden with herring, for London. A couple hours after she had left harbour she struck on the Barnard sands, and went to pieces in just five minutes. The lifeboat arrived too late to save the crew and all three were found drowned. The vessel at the time was reported to have been ninety years old.

On Saturday 11th February 1871, in the afternoon the brig "Ann & Elizabeth", Lenman, of Fowey, from Middlesbrough, for Briton Ferry, with pig iron, and while passing through the Stanford Channel, struck on a wreck on the outside of the Newcome Sand. On seeing this Robert mustered a crew and launched the yawl "Happy New Year" and rescued the crew, landing them and received at the Sailors Home. As she had all sails set when abandoned, she was forced over the sand with her bows under, and would later sink in deep water. A portion of wreck, with the quarter-board painted blue, supposed to belong to the above brig, was afterwards picked up at Pakefield.

The annual proceedings in connection with the Suffolk Humane Society and the Lowestoft and Pakefield Lifeboat Society took place on Wednesday 23rd August 1871, in the presence of a large concourse of spectators, to many of whom they were a novelty, and coxswain Hook and crew afforded consequently the greater pleasure and interest. At eleven o'clock the boats were afloat for the inspection of subscribers, visitors, and the public. The Lowestoft Lifeboat was brought alongside the south-pier, and numerous were the applications from visitors-wishing to be able to say, on their return home, that they had a trip seaward in a Lifeboat, Robert just asked for a donation for the Lifeboat fund for a berth on board her. The morning was lovely for a sail, a beautiful breeze having sprung up from the South-West., just before starting. This caused some to leave the boat, fearing, I suppose, the unpleasant consequences of the heaving waves. One or two gentlemen on leaving said the seat had only been taken just to be able to say, "they had been in a Lifeboat". The boat having left the harbour proceeded southerly, and for the Newcome Sand, subsequently returning to the starting point to take another live cargo, for the same purpose as the last. The amateur mariners behaved very well upon the whole and were gratified with the excursion.

On Wednesday 13th November 1872 Hook who was on
watch observed flares from a vessel having difficulty near the
Corton patch, this vessel turned out to be the Norwegian brig
Expedite sailing from London with fire wood and telegraph
poles. As soon as the crew could be mustered, 19 beach-men
in total the Laetitia was launched under the coxswain Robert.
Hook, in addition Mr. John. Henderson, chief officer of the
coast guard, procceeded in tow by the harbour tug
personally commanded by the harbour master, Captain
Massingham. The wind was a moderate gale from the N.E,
and on approaching found the brig to be on the north point
of the Holm Sand, dismasted, and the raffle hanging
alongside making it very dangerous to get near her. The
lifeboat dropped her anchor and attempted to get near the

brig, The Lifeboat was hit by heavy wave after heavy wave entangling her in the rigging from the brig in the surrounding water. Having freed herself, it was with great difficulty and risk that the Lifeboat crew got alongside, and one by one the ten hands jumped into the Lifeboat from their precarious position.

It was reported in the local paper that while returning under tow the entire fish docks turned out to cheer the returning hero's and the rescued crew from the brig. They were taken to the sailors Home, where they received all the attention they required including fresh clothes. "We regret that in connection with this noble deed, and which we hope will bring the gallant coxswain a gold medal, we have to report that one of the waves encountered by the Lifeboat brought down her foreyard, which, falling upon one of her crew named Harry Hall, broke his leg; but which was not known to several on board her until the poor fellow got into the harbour. He was removed as quickly as possible to the infirmary, where he received the immediate attention of Frank Worthington, Esq., and other officials of that institution". A subscription on his behalf was started.

On Tuesday 18th March 1873, the schooner "Celine" of and from Gravelines, when ashore on the Holm Sand, about eleven o'clock in the morning, while the wind was blowing fresh from the north-east and a heavy sea was running. The Lowestoft large lifeboat of the National Institution went off to the wreck and found it full of water. Fortunately, the lifeboat was successful in saving six of the shipwrecked crew, but the master could not be got to leave the vessel, and the men had to leave without him, and had to cut the lifeboat's cable to enable her to clear the ship.

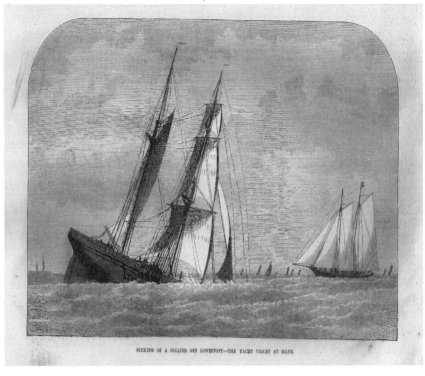

SINKING OF A COLLIER OFF LOWESTOFT—THE YACHT VIOLET AT HAND.

On Wednesday October 2nd, 1873 the Lifeboat Institution held their usual quarterly meeting of the committee of the Lowestoft, Pakefield, and Corton branch of the above Institution, was held at the Court house to receive the reports for the last quarter. Mr. G. Edwards, Esq., J.P, occupied the chair. After the minutes of the previous meeting had been read and confirmed, reference was made to the loss of the Norfolk Lass, on the Corton Sand, on the

22nd August 1873. The secretary stated that a good deal of stories had been circulating in the press about it, but no blame was laid against the Lifeboat crew, although surprise had been expressed that no Lifeboat was launched. Robert Hook explained that due to it being regatta day in Lowestoft he was unable to muster a full crew and due to the tide being against them the steam tug would have been required to tow them out, and besides the Gorleston Lifeboat had gone to her aid as they were much closer, and the subject was dropped. It was decided to get out the large boat, No 1, for the winter, and also No 2 to be got ready for any emergency. It was also decided to move the Lifeboat shed at Corton more to the North, in order to be more convenient for the men if required. The meeting was then adjourned.

On Saturday 29th November 1873, the large screw- steamer named the "Columbo," of and for Hull, with a valuable cargo from Alexandria, was that morning on the Barnard-Sands, off Lowestoft. The Old Company beach-men were employed to try and save the vessel. The cargo was unloaded to lighten her, so she could be pulled off and be refloated.

On Friday morning of the 11th December 1874, a strong gale prevailed off the eastern coast from the S.S.E., and all the vessels which were riding in the Lowestoft Roads were being watched with intense anxiety. Just before 10.am; a large ketch was observed to part from her anchor and drove towards the beach. As she neared the beach the excitement of the spectators was increased when someone pointed out that there was a woman lashed to the rigging some height above the deck. The ketch beached opposite the Royal Hotel. The breakers were so heavy that it was too extremely dangerous to get near her on foot, and yet there was not sufficient depth of water to float a boat; in fact, the water between the dry portion of beach and the vessel was all surf. The wind increased in force, and was accompanied with heavy rain. The heavy breakers washed over the ketch's decks, completely enveloping the crew in mist. A runner was dispatched to the coast-guard station for the rocket apparatus, which was quickly brought to the promenade and fired in full view of Titan. In the mean while the gallant beach-men made desperate efforts to get to the vessel, in order to bring the women ashore. At last a number of men formed a chain by grasping each other's hands, and the one nearest the ketch succeeded in throwing a rope, by which he and a second man hauled themselves to the deck. They then ascended the rigging, brought the women down, and dropped her over the side of the vessel, where the brave men stood in the sea mist of the breakers, and got her ashore, amid the acclamations of the bye-standers. Mr. W.H.Aldred, who lived on the esplanade, was standing by with a blanket and a flask of brandy, and gave a shot of stimulant to the semi-delirious woman. She was then taken to the Sailors Home. The Coastguard under the direction of Mr.Henderson; set to work rescuing the ketch's crew, the four hands were brought ashore using the cradle. The ketch was the "Argo," of Goole, Brown, master, for Maldon with wheat. While the crew of the ketch were being rescued, at the same time Robert Hook and fellow Lifeboat crew members were fully occupied in the rescue of the crew of a fine schooner. About half a mile away from the spot where the "Argo," laid, was a fine schooner in a more perilous position than the ketch, because the beach there is more-steep, and the billows rolled over the schooner in great volume. The bulwarks on one side of the vessel had been torn away, and those on the starboard side of the vessel were partly gone. The Lifeboat crew commenced the tedious work of launching a surf Lifeboat. While the Lifeboat was being launched, the number of spectators increased to several thousand. The anxiety was intensified by seeing one of the crew preparing to jump overboard. On hearing the shouts of some of the beach-men, who ran into the breakers as far as it was possible, the man pulled himself back under the bulwark railing. The vessel rolled so tremendously that it was feared that the main-mast, with its yards and rigging, would fall upon the crew. It was a question also whether it was prudent to attempt to get the Lifeboat alongside the vessel while the vessel lurched so heavily. Presently she filled with water and became steadier, and efforts were renewed for floating the Lifeboat. At this moment one of the crew jumped from the schooner into the surf. He was evidently a good swimmer, and struggled with vigour. The receding waves were the stronger, and the beach-men and on-lookers were certain he would not be able to reach land unaided. He gained a momentary footing once, and stood up, but was quickly knocked down. Several beach-men, without holding any rope ran into the surf as far as they dared, but failed to reach the struggling man. The coxswain Robert Hook secured a rope around his waist and walked into the surf, then went up to his chin and firmly grasped the drowning man, and brought him within the reach of others, who quickly rescued him from danger. Ultimately the Lifeboat was got alongside the schooner, and the jumping of the crew into the Lifeboat was followed by loud hurrahs by the crowd on the beach. The Lifeboat was quickly hauled ashore by hundreds of volunteers. The schooner was the "Lady Basset," Brook, master, of Teignmouth, from Runcorn for Newcastle, with salt.

On the 14th January 1876, the Laetitia was now twenty-six years old and this was her final service. While passing Corton on her way from Shields to her home-port, the three-mast schooner "George-Smeed," of Rochester lost her foremast. Robert Hook on seeing her distress flares, launched the Lifeboat and was followed by the harbour tug. The Lifeboat escorted the schooner into Lowestoft while it was under tow by the harbour tug.

On Wednesday 13th September 1876 an inquest was held at the Masonic hall by C.W. Cheston.Esq, county coroner, regarding the death of William Lewis, aged 44 years. As it was an inquest the evidence was given in detail. James Shelley said: "I am master of a smack and live at Lowestoft."I found the body of the deceased yesterday morning about 6am, in the inner harbour. "I pulled it out of the water and with assistance conveyed it to the dead house."There were marks upon his face as if the deceased had fallen upon something. "I found the body in 2 feet of water.

John Butcher, beach-man, Lowestoft said: "I knew the deceased William Lewis." I last saw him alive at the Fisherman's Arms a beer house on the beach, kept by coxswain of the Lifeboat Robert Hook, on Saturday the 2nd of September. "He appeared sober." I have viewed the body and recognize it as William Lewis. "The deceased told me he belonged to the Dreadnought".

William King ship agent, Lowestoft, said: "I'am the agent for the Dreadnought, "I knew the deceased: he was one of the crew, "The Dreadnought sailed from Lowestoft on Tuesday the 5th, without the deceased, as according to the captain's report, he was away drinking." "The captain sailed with the clothes of the deceased on board, being recommend doing so by the shipping master, as he was regarded as a deserter." "I saw him after the ship sailed; I think it was on the Thursday." He was walking in Commercial Road." I have viewed the body and am certain it is the same man."

Samuel Chamberlain, bridge-man. Lowestoft, said: "I saw a man who was missing from the Dreadnought, on Wednesday night, the 6th, about 10pm, standing against Mr Perrett's, the chemist, but I was not close enough to notice if he was sober or drunk. He came out of the harbour inn just before."

Mr.W.H.Clubbe, surgeon, Lowestoft said: "I saw the body of the deceased at the dead-house at 5pm yesterday. Putrefaction had set in to such an extent as to remove the usual external appearance of death from drowning, if they ever existed. Blood was flowing from the nostrils and there were several marks on the face which seemed to have been caused after death by rats, or crabs or other fish. I never saw a body decomposed that bad, as it had only been in the water four days. From the external examination it is impossible to say the cause of death". The jury returned a verdict of death from "some unknown cause, being found dead in the water of the inner harbour, and there being no evidence to show the cause of death".

On Thursday 21st December 1876 at Sparham's boat building yard on the North beach at Lowestoft. The Samuel Plimsoll Lifeboat, subscribed for by the Plimsoll Lifeboat Fund committee at Derby and Liverpool, was launched in the presence of several thousand spectators and the existing lifeboat crew. The Lifeboat is 44 feet long, 12 feet wide, and pulls 14 oars. Rear-Admiral Mac-donald, in a suitable speech, received the boat on behalf of the Royal National Lifeboat Institution, and Mr.Plimsoll.M.P., delivered a short address, in which he said that, notwithstanding all that had been done to prevent unseaworthy ships being sent to sea, there must always remain a certain margin of inevitable disaster which necessitated the existence of Lifeboat Institutions. He added: - I was staying some-time ago down at Sizewell, when I was much struck with the magnificent feeling of the men who manned the boats. A friend of mine told me that he was down on the beach on one occasion when the boat was launched, and the men afterwards found that they had forgotten the nightlights. When the boat got into the offing or into the bank the men could not show by a light that they were safe, nor could they get to the vessel in peril, as the sea was so rough. The men therefore, kept out all night, but I believe that the lifeboat from this station went to the wreck and succeeded, with the aid of the Sizewell boat, in saving 14 men. (Applause.) Instead of bemoaning the hardships they had to endure for some had gone off without their jerseys and without their cork jackets- the only feeling expressed was one of disappointment that they had not got the biggest share of the men who were saved- for they had got only three while the other boat got eleven. (Applause, and cries of "We know that.") That was a magnificent thing, and it seemed to me as if there was a sort of sporting feeling among the men. Whereas the officers of our army in India boast that they had shot elephants and brought down tigers, these sailors and beach-men can boast that they have saved so many lives. That is a grand boast, and it delights me to hear it. (Applause.)- Mr.J.J.Colman, M.P., expressed the pleasure with which the Local Committee received the Lifeboat, associated as it was with such a worthy name.

The first real loss of the season occurred on Wednesday 7th November 1877, under the following circumstances. It appears that about 2 a.m., signal flares were to be observed in the neighbourhood of the South Newcome-Sand, Hook was on look out at the Old Company shed and witnessed the distress signals. Hook rounded up his crew and prepared the Lifeboat for launching, at this point James Peek arrived at the lifeboat shed to inform them it was the Lugger "Pet," which had struck the sand and he had just left them and travelled back to raise the alarm in his yawl. The new Samuel Plimsol Lifeboat was launched to the wreck, and after two hours work, had the great satisfaction of landing her crew of eleven hands and one dog in Lowestoft harbour. Hook the coxswain told the press that, "the men on the Pet were ready for any emergency, and had almost given up hope, having bowls around their waists, and their frocks filled with cork." The night was very wild and dirty, and the darkness such as could almost be felt, but nothing caused the men of the Lifeboat to swerve from their duty to rescue their fellow-creatures.

On Wednesday 2nd October 1878, the usual quarterly meeting of the committee of the Lowestoft, Pakefield and Corton branch of the Lifeboat Institution, was held at the Court House, to receive the reports for the past quarter. G. Edwards, Esq. J.P., occupied the chair, and there were present W.F.Larkins, W. Cole, B. Preston, J.Henderson, and the Secretary, Mr.F.Morse. After the minutes of the previous meeting had been read and confirmed, reference was made to the loss of the "Norfolk Lass", on Corton Sand, on the 22nd of August. The secretary stated that a good deal of correspondence had taken place about it, but no blame was laid against their Lifeboat crews, although surprise has been excited that no boat had gone off. He also stated he had received letters from J.J.Colman, Esq., M.P., and the secretaries to the Gorleston Lifeboat Committee and the Trinity Company. Mr.Henderson explained that it was the regatta day, and that there was some difficulty in getting the men to go off in the Lifeboat, and there were not enough to man the large boat, and that had there been they could not have got to the scene of the wreck till nearly one o'clock, as they would have wanted the tug to have towed the boat with, the wind and tide being against her. Beside the Gorleston Lifeboat, which did go to the vessel, and which was so much nearer, could render her no service. Robert Hook, coxswain, explained the circumstances of the case as far as he and his men were concerned, and expressed a similar opinion to Mr.Henderson, and the subject dropped. It was decided to get out the large boat, No.1, for the winter, and also No.2 to be got ready for any emergency. The Lifeboat shed at Corton, it was said, it was proposed to be moved more to the North, in order to be more convenient for the men if required, and after the transaction of some routine business, the meeting adjourned.

On Sunday 10th November 1878, the Samuel Plimsoll Lifeboat, belonging to the National Lifeboat Institution, performed this morning a noble service in saving a shipwrecked crew of 21 hands. The screw steamer "Yorin," from Riga to London, with Oats, struck early that morning on the dangerous Holm-Sand. Without delay the coxswain Bob Hook, on the signal of distress being observed, roused his crew from their beds. They at once launched the boat, and brought ashore in two hours afterwards the shipwrecked crew. On the weather moderating, attempts were made by a steam tug and the lifeboat to get the steamer off the sands; this was fortunately accomplished, and the steamer was brought safely into harbour.

A strong gale prevailed in Lowestoft on Thursday 28th November 1878, and the brigantine "Zosteria," Robert.J.Crosby master, of Colchester, from Poole for Middlesbrough, with railway iron, brought up under shelter of Holm-Sand. At 8p.m., the wind increased, and the roll of the waves caused his cargo to shift from one side to the other. The master set off distress flares for assistance, and at 11p.m., a steam tug, with the Lowestoft Lifeboat (Samuel Plimsoll) in tow, arrived alongside. The crew of the "Zosteria" wished the Lifeboat to remain alongside till daylight, but Robert Hook, coxswain of the lifeboat refused, and said" I will take you and your master now or leave, it's up to you, if you want to put your cargo before your own lives, but i will not risk my crew." The master deeded it prudent to leave the vessel, as at any moment the loose iron might go through her, his crew of four hands got into the lifeboat and they were towed into Lowestoft by the steam tug and received at the sailor's home. The following day the tug towed the "Zosteria" into harbour.

A special meeting of the committee of the Lowestoft and Pakefield branch of the National Lifeboat Institution was held at the Court House on Wednesday 26th January 1881, in the afternoon, to take into consideration communications received from Mr.J.Robertson, collector of customs at Lowestoft, and Mr.R.Lewis, secretary to the Lifeboat Institution. It appears that on Thursday subsequent to the fearful gale of the 18th January, a telegram was received at 7.42 a.m., by captain Massingham harbour master, from Capt. Haward, the marine superintendent at Harwich, stated that the "Avalon (s.s) had been obliged to slip from an Italian barque, which was drifting up towards the ship-wash; crew on board, vessel dismasted, and inquired whether Capt.Massingham could come with the tug and Lifeboat. To this, after he had consulted with Robert Hook, coxswain of the Lifeboat, he consented, and the tug and lifeboat left at 9a.m., and arrived at the ships-wash at 12 o'clock, and from information he received he went to the cutter buoy, where he saw the barque in tow of one of the Hewitts steam carriers. He hailed the barque, which was making a great deal of water, and inquired whether they required any assistance, which was declined, Hook anyway sent three to four of the Lifeboat crew on board to see if they could render any help, but they were not needed. Captain Massingham then went to Harwich, and while there the Harwich Lifeboat went off and rescued seven men from a wreck several miles off. Captain Massingham returned with the Lifeboat in tow on Friday afternoon at about three o'clock, on what turned out to be a pointless folly. Hook told the committee at no point was shipping at Lowestoft at risk, because they left behind three Lifeboats, Corton, Pakefield and Lowestoft No2 boat, with that the committee adjourned.

On March 7th, Robert Hook and his crew rendered service to the smack "Alert", which was grounded off Lowestoft, and the beach-men went in their yawl to the smack, but could not get sufficiently near to rescue the distressed crew. The beach-men returned with their yawl, and then went out in the Lowestoft Lifeboat. On reaching the "Alert" a second time the Lowestoft crew discovered that the Pakefield Lifeboat had taken the crew off the wreck.

On March 17th, 1881 Robert Hook, Robert's father died at the ripe old age of 85 years.

On March 22nd the local Committee met, firstly they passed on their condolences to the coxswain for the loss of his father and then turned attention to the service rendered to the "Alert" on the 7th. After hearing the fact's, the committee did not feel justified in recommending the parent Committee to pay the full reward to the Lowestoft crew, but only for the exercised service the amount awarded was £8.16s., and the Lowestoft crew told the committee what they could do with it, so it was refused.

On October 28th, 1882, a day still remembered as "Black Saturday" by many an old hand in Lowestoft occurred. On the 27th it started off as a mild day and then turned to rain and by Saturday the weather had turned into a howling gale, with a raging tide and heavy swell. That afternoon on the Saturday many boats in the roads of lowestoft had flags of distress, but newspapers would say the Lifeboat failed to launch due to grievances as to payments for some recent launches. "Let them as rob the crew save the lives" was the reply to protests. By the evening other ships and boats had distress flags and crew in the riggings a total of twenty was mentioned in the papers between Yarmouth and Southwold, and the papers said lives had already been lost. An angry mob of by-standers accosted Hook and his crew as they returned to the boat house, papers at the time had Robert and his crew skulking around the stove in the boatshed and fail to mention that Hook and his men were dripping sodden wet after spending the whole day saving lives with the smaller beach yawls. They called for Hook to unlock the doors and launch the Lifeboat and if he didn't they would show him and his crew up in the country's papers as cowards. To be fair the beach-man who considered themselves no longer to be members of the Lifeboat crew after a disagreement earlier that year, that morning Hook and his fellow beach-man had been assisting vessels which had made a run for the safety of the harbour, helping them through the pier-heads and mooring them; they had also been helping to get crew off the ships that had went aground on the beach when they missed the harbour entrance.

The Coastguard by the means of the rocket apparatus saved the crew of the collier "Messenger", of Blyth, along with a group of beach-men who were trying to get her of the beach just south of the harbour entrance, then soon after 6pm three further collier brigs were driven ashore and beached. Soon after 6pm another three collier brigs ran aground on the beach as they attempted to enter the harbour. The Mornington, of Colchester and the Susanna Dixon, of Whitby, then the Isis, of Cowes, broke free from her anchor and ploughed into the Susanna Dixon.

The Pakefield Lifeboat just watched as the coastguard used their rocket apparatus to try and save the crew of the brigantine William Thrift which had been grounded opposite the Pakefield boathouse, but it became clear that the 14 men in the rigging could only be saved by the lifeboat. Robert Hook and the beach-men at that point were rescuing the captain, his wife and three children and crew from the ketch Q.E.D., of Dartmouth, which was beached just opposite the gasworks. Further beach-men assisted with saving the crews of the schooner Prosper, of Caernarvon, and the schooner Launceston, of Fowey; George Hall an owner of a local smack, received a silver medal from the RNLI for going out to the Prosper to the aid of a elderly sailor in his seventy's and that was the point the mob accosted Hook at the Boathouse. Robert Hook did go and unlock the lifeboat boathouse but launching the boat was no easy matter as the wreck of the Q.E.D. was right in front of the boathouse and moving a lifeboat weighing in at ten tons required at least 100 men to move to the water.

The smaller lifeboat arrived at the William thrift and collected the seventeen men in the rigging, the next day she when out to help bring in the ketch Evening Star, of Hull, which was badly damaged in the previous night's gales.

On November 14th, 1882 were published the results of the inquiry into the circumstances connected with the delay in launching the Lowestoft Lifeboat during the gales which occurred on the eastern coast on the 28th of October. The inquiry which occupied three days, was conducted by Captain the Hon.H.W.Chetwynd.R.N., and Commander Vincent Nepean. R.N., Inspectors of Lifeboats to the Royal National Lifeboat Institution, and on Friday 7th Nov their report was presented at a crowded public meeting held at Lowestoft under the presidency of the rector. This report occasions more regret than surprise, for censure is cast not only on Robert Hook, the coxswain of the Lowestoft Lifeboat, who for a time positively refused to launch it, but ultimately did all he could to assist in saving the drowning seamen, but also on the Hon.Superintendent (Mr. Henderson) and the Hon. Secretary (Mr. Morse), for misconception or neglect of duty. It appears to be admitted the Lifeboat crew had a substantial grievance with respect to a service rendered to a vessel called the "Alert" on the 7th march 1882, for which they were awarded the sum of £8 16s,but refused the grant, claiming the full night service money,£24. Mr. Henderson appears to have acquainted Mr.Lewis, the secretary of the Institution, with the refusal, which was stoutly persisted in; indeed, in May the money was returned by Mr. Henderson to London. In Consequence of the dissatisfaction thus occasioned the crew refusing to have anything further to do with the Lifeboat, and in June Captain Nepean reported that Mr. Henderson expected trouble whenever they might be required. It does not appear, however, that the authority in London took any steps to obviate the dangers of this position, and some explanation of their actions are due to the public. The evidence given at the inquiry about the above rescue in March is as follows; Robert hook; "we launched the boat and went to the vessel. It was March, I believe. We saved no lives. "You never received your shares of the money paid for that service", Hook "Not a penny". "Then my reply will be an application to the parent Institution for the men's receipt for the money. What is the arrangement of you the coxswain stopping the 4d? Hook "That's an old rule and custom; but we people who don't drink the beer are not supposed to have the 4d, cut off." If you don't drink it do the others get it? Hook "I suppose no".

Are you tea-total? -"Hook" No, but I have not drunk any beer for four years. (Laughter from the public gallery.) I have tried to alter the custom". The Chairman replied, "The majority liked the beer best". Hook explained that "the beer money was an old and legal custom ", "in regards to the Alert, the money had been shared. So also had the money for the progress been shared".

William Capps, beach-man, and one of the lifeboat crew, gave similar evidence. The report expressed an opinion that the beach-men had cause of complaint and were fairly entitled to pay for night service, and that no greater responsibility rested on them with respect to manning the lifeboat on the 28th of October than on the rest of the seafaring population present on the beach; but the report said that is different with coxswain Hook, whose neglect of duty on this occasion is, said the report, the more to be regretted after a series of gallant services performed during a period of over thirty years, and for which he had received the Institutions silver medal and second service clasp. But William Cooper (North road company) in his evidence given at the inquiry stated ", I never saw anyone on Saturday refuse to launch the lifeboat, that includes our coxswain Hook. The only time I remember Hook ever refusing to launch was five years ago, at the wreck of the Harry and Ernest". Hook replied, "if I remember on that occasion we went out at once".

Back to the report and Captain Nepean himself comes in for a share of the blame, for having insufficiently examined the haul off wrap, which broke more than once under the strain put upon it by the beach-men. The report refers in very cordial terms to the actions taken by two visitors, Mr. W.M.Hazard, of Harleston, and Mr. Gilbert Stracey, each of who offered a pound a head to any who would man the lifeboat, the evidence stated at the inquiry was as follows; Mr. Hazard said "I sent a man named Ambler to the coxswain, but the man returned saying that Hook refused to come or let the boat go. When I got to their boathouse I saw Hook leaning against the wall smoking his pipe in his shirt sleeves. I said men were drowning within sight and hearing of the harbour; and told him if he did not let the boat go off it was as much as murder as if he stuck a knife into them. Hook refused to go and said the key was in the boat house door, or it was unlocked. "I heard the men talking of grievances, but I told the men to put them to one side, and that money should be no object. I said I would give a pound a head to the men to launch the boat, and Mr. Gilbert Stracey, who was present, said he would give a pound too. It was stated in the papers that I paid £30 to the crew who went off: but I wish to say Mr. Gilbert Stracey paid half with me. (Applause) Hook used strong language to me; but his justification was, I suppose, that I had called him as bad as a murderer. I told him I would smash open the boat house doors, Hook said the boat weighed ten tons, and could not be launched. I sent to the pier for volunteers, and we had plenty of men to launch the boat and man her. There must have been 500 to 1000 people on the beach then, Hook took his money when I paid the other men who had manned the boat.

Mr. Symes, the chief officer of the coastguard, in the course
of his evidence, observed, amidst cheers, that during the
gales Hook had already saved 25 lives.

THE ILLUSTRATED LONDON NEWS, Nov. 11, 1862.—492

1. Life-boat to the rescue. 2. Signals for help. 3. Towing in a disabled vessel. 4. Duly striking the North Pier. 5. On Pakefield Beach. 6. Morning after the gale.

SKETCHES DURING THE GALE AT LOWESTOFT.

Back to the report and with respect to the two Pakefield lifeboats, the report stated that one was not launched in consequence of a misunderstanding on the part of the coxswain as to instructions given on a previous occasion by one of the committee; the other boat made every possible effort to render service, but was driven back by the irresistible force of wind and sea. The inquiry appeared to

164

have been an honest and searching one, and would be the means of preventing the recurrence of such a harrowing scene as what was witnessed on Lowestoft Beach that night.

On Tuesday November 14h 1882, the Lowestoft Lifeboat crew and their coxswain Robert Hook performed another daring and gallant rescue which was hoped to wipe out the remembrance of the recent events. The reverend T.A.Nash, Rector of Lowestoft, wrote to the Times with the following: - "As I feel that one authentic case of distinguished bravery is worth a thousand denials of the charge of fear or cowardice I ask you to allow me to relate what happened today. About eight o'clock this morning the Norwegian Brig Berthon, laden with timber, struck the sands opposite Lowestoft. She was soon in the surf and the sea making a clean sweep over her. The crew of eight men were seen from the shore clinging with the grip of death to her rigging. The Lifeboat, by the aid of the steam-tug, was soon on her way to the rescue under the charge of Robert Hook. When within half a mile of the wreck the sails of the boat were hoisted, and away she went with the direction of an arrow into the surf. Wave after wave fell upon her, and the crew had to hold on for very life, fearing they might be washed out of her: but life to them at that moment was worth the risking if only they might save the half-drowned sailors. Clever seamanship brought the Lifeboat just at the needed moment, and one after another of the sailors were got into the Lifeboat. In just 15min not a timber could be seen of the wreck. The rescue came only in time, so soon did the vessel break up. As we watched the

Lifeboat from the shore, it seemed as if she went again and again right under the water. The promptness and desperate daring of the rescue are this afternoon the subject of universal praise.

Hook, in telling me about it, said "The saving of that crew is worth to me more than £100: it seems as if an Almighty power sent it in our time of trouble."

Pakefield, too, has got its answer to the world. This morning at five o'clock the brig Widgeon went on the sands. The Lifeboat was soon in the furious waters, but the situation of the vessel rendered it impossible to rescue the sailors. Again and again the noble lifeboat men literally fought the waves and were driven back, and in the last effort three of the men were washed out of the Lifeboat; two of them recovered by the lifeboat, but the coxswain Warford, was washed ashore, bruised, and half dead. The sailors were ultimately saved by the rocket apparatus under Mr. Symer.

"I ask you, Sir, to kindly insert this letter as a proof to the world that want of courage or readiness to risk life for the purpose of saving others had nothing to do with the unhappy matter alluding to (referring to black Saturday). The court of inquiry has issued its report and the public can form their opinion upon it, but I want to deliver a brave race of men from a charge of want of bravery, a bravery which is expected of them, but which is often too feebly recognized and too little rewarded. As I write this the Newcome claims another, crew off again to a steamer and a scotch boat on the sands. "May God help stout hearts and strong arms in the rescue".

On Tuesday 14th November 1882, the brig "Harkaway," of Shoreham, from Newhaven, for Hartlepool, was riding in Lowestoft roads in the afternoon. The master Mr.Light on seeing that his hold was taking on water raised signals of distress. The Lifeboat was towed out by the harbour tug and succeeded in bringing in the crew and schooner into Lowestoft harbour. In addition to the "Harkaway" the brig "Wilhelmina" was also towed in shortly after, with the lifeboat standing by.

On Wednesday 15th November 1882, between 2 and 3am in the morning, in answer to flares, the Lowestoft Lifeboat proceeded to a vessel lying in the South-Roads, which proved to be the schooner "Jane," of Faversham. One boy and man left the brig and got into the Lifeboat. The wind having considerably moderated, the other portion of crew would not leave the vessel. At daylight the schooner was not to be seen at Lowestoft and it was supposed she had sailed for Harwich.

The very splendid service rendered by the Lowestoft Lifeboat and the attempted service by the Pakefield Lifeboat on Tuesday incited a few gentlemen to collect donations to present to the crew. On Wednesday 15th November in the evening, at the Harbour Hotel, at a meeting of a portion of the donors, Capt. Thomas Bennett presented to Robert Hook, the coxswain of the Lowestoft Lifeboat, £27.9s.2d for the crew, for the splendid service rendered in saving the crew of eight hands of the barque "Berthon," of Norway. Hook stated "I believe that whatever brave service is required it would be quickly rendered by this crew." The Reverend J.Tracy, who watched the service through a telescope, described the bravery of the Lifeboat crew as marvellous. The sea was breaking over the sand with terrific force, and for several minutes it appeared that the wreck would be washed into the Lifeboat. Coxswain Hook, acknowledged, and said "Captain Porter, of the steam-tug, in my opinion deserves the greatest praise for towing the Lifeboat as he did." John Peek, of the Pakefield Lifeboat, received £13.7s.6d for his crew, and £2 was retained for the two who rescued Coxswain Warford. The total amount contributed was £43.3s.6d, which included one guinea collected by the men of the Lowestoft Artillery Volunteers at the drill hall that evening. Thanks were accorded to Captain Bennett for presiding. With referance to coxswain Warford, he took out the Pakefield Lifeboat to the brig "Widgeon," of Blyth, but due to the rough sea he and two other men were washed overboard.

On the 22nd November 1882, A meeting was held and chaired by the Reverend T.A.Nash, it was attended by Hook and his crew, Captain Massingham (Harbour Master), Captain Porter (Master of the Dispatch), and others. Nash spoke about the bravery of Robert and his crew and wished that some sort of recognition to be given. Mr Seago had arranged a collection for funds to have a medal struck in the form of a Maltese-Cross inscribed "The crew of the Berthon rescued Nov.14th 1882". On the reverse side it was inscribed with the recipient's name and presented in a morocco leather and silk lined case. The idea for the medal came from a letter published in the Lowestoft Journal who signed himself as Whistling Willie and stated to be acquainted with the crew and was sure he and the crew would be proud to wear a medal. Some people thought that this might have been Robert Hook writing in under an assumed name. But however the medal were struck by E F Crake of Lowestoft.

The International Fisheries Exhibition at South Kensington was opened on Saturday 12th May 1883, by the Prince of Wales, by the command of the Queen, who would have performed the ceremony herself had it not been that she still suffers from the effects of her recent accident. The scene within the exhibition building at the opening ceremony was of the most brilliant character. About 400 men from Great Britain and Ireland, of which ten men from Lowestoft's fishermen formed one of the contingents. The 400 fishermen arrived in London on Friday from the various parts of the country and were met at the railway station, if desired, and conducted to the Sailors-Home, Well Street, Poplar. Saturday was the opening of this exhibition, and the men assembled in a specially constructed building, being drawn up in double line facing inwards, and through this line the procession passed. The Lowestoft men formed the right hand company, and were much admired by all spectators, not simply on account of their characteristic and uniform costume, but also their grand physique and manly bearing. Monday was devoted to the exhibition. On Tuesday morning the men were entertained at the Fishmongers-Hall, and went again to the exhibition. Wednesday the fishermen were inspected in the morning together with the North Country fishwives at Marlborough House, and most graciously received by their Royal Highnesses the prince and princess of Wales at luncheon. By command of the Queen they proceeded to Windsor Castle in the afternoon to view the state apartments and other objects of interest. They were regaled with an excellent dinner in the riding school, and returned to town delighted with their visit. It was an unfortunate circumstance that the state of Her Majesty's health prevented a personal inspection of a body of men unequalled in their loyalty and attachment to the Royal House. On the way back from Windsor the Lowestoft fishermen along with the others were invited to be entertained by the Lord Mayor, at the Mansion House. They were most kindly and warmly received by the Lord and Lady Mayoress. The saloons were thrown open and lighted up with the electric light, and various objects of value shown to the men such as the historic civic plate, the state ropes, paintings, armour, statuary, Etc. The Lord Mayor asked Robert Hook to take the Lady Mayoress into the Egyptian Hall to refreshments, and she was much impressed by the graceful manner he performed this agreeable duty. Her Ladyship gave Hook a photograph of herself and the Lord Mayor expressed the pleasure it would afford her to give place in her album to the portrait of a man who has rendered such good cause to humanity, by being instrumental in saving no less than 600 lives from shipwreck.

ROBERT HOOK
THE LOWESTOFT HERO
WHO HAS SAVED OVER 600 LIVES

After the fishwives and fishermen had been refreshed, music and dancing ensued, the Lord Mayor leading off a Scotch reel with one of the Newhaven women. The following morning a deputation of fishermen, Robert. Hook for England, a Baniffshire man for Scotland, and a lively young Roscommon fellow for Ireland to present a beautiful bouquet of choice flowers to the Lady Mayoress, in rememberance of the hospitality at the Mansion House the previous evening.

In January 1884 it became time for Robert Hook to call time on the Fisherman's arms, after years of pulling pints for his fellow beach-men it went on the market In the Ipswich journal it was described as; Lot 6."The Fisherman's Arms," a well know BEERHOUSE, situated on Whapload-road, in the occupation of Mr.Robert W.Hook, at the yearly rent of £30. Roll on 110 years and when I had my pub in Ipswich called the "Old Times", my yearly rent was £12,000 per year what a difference? But never the less Robert stayed on a further ten years.

Lowestoft Foreshore Case; Robert Hook was called to give evidence in the High Court of Justice, the case of the Attorney-General V Richard Henry Reeve was tried on Wednesday 10th June 1885. It was an information filed by the Attorney-General on behalf of the Crown, and the application was to have the title of the Crown declared to a portion of the Foreshore at Lowestoft, which was claimed by the defendant as Lord of the Manor. The information set out various Acts of Parliament passed for the purpose of constructing, maintaining, and improving the Harbour at Lowestoft. In which undertaking the Great Eastern Railway Company had now become interested, and detailed some indentures by which that the Company had become entitled, by Grants from the Crown, to remove shingle at 2d.per ton from the Foreshore for the ballasting vessels coming into Lowestoft Harbour. The place from which the Company removed shingle adjoined that portion of the Foreshore claimed by the defendant. In consequence of the construction of the harbour and the works connected therewith, the sea had receded at a certain point adjoining the manor, and the defendant claimed, as Lord of the Manor, to be entitled to the piece of Foreshore so left uncovered. It was further alleged that the recession of the sea from time to time had been perceptible in its progress, and that being the case it was contended by the law of the land the foreshore in question became the property of the crown. Recently the Great Eastern Railway Company required another piece of foreshore from which to take shingle for the purpose of their undertaking, and the Company had commenced negotiations with the crown for the purchase, but as the defendant set up his claim the company declined to complete the purchase pending the establishment of the title of the Crown to the Foreshore in question. Besides, therefore, praying to have their title declared, the crown asked the defendant might be restrained from continuing the proceedings against the railway company under the Lands Clauses Consolidation Act, which he had started for the purpose of obtaining compensation from the company for the taking away of shingle. The defendant, in his answer, said that he was Lord of the Manor of Lowestoft, having acquired the title under an indenture from Sir Samuel Morton Peto; and that the point of high water mark at and near the point in question had altered considerably within living memory, and more rapidly in recent years since the construction of the works referred to; that in some portions, and particularly at a place called Ness-Point, the sea had encroached largely upon the manor, whilst at other points, including the disputed piece of foreshore, the sea had receded to about the same extent, but not wholly, to the construction of the said works; That since he had been lord of the manor he had, and to the best of his knowledge and belief his predecessors in title had always exercised, from time to time, rights and acts of ownership over the foreshore; that he did not claim to be owner of any part of the foreshore which now lay, or which hereafter might lie between high and low water marks of ordinary tides, but he claimed all such lands as were now, or might hereafter be landward of high-water mark of ordinary tides, whenever such high-water mark was from time to time shifted by the gradual and imperceptible action of the sea, whether such shifting was wholly due to natural causes or to artifical works, and he claimed the accreted land in question as having formed by the slow, gradual, and imperceptible retirement of the sea. Evidence, which was in the form of affidavits, was then read. Mr Arthur.R.Fairfield, first clerk in the office of the board of trade; Mr.James.Frazer.Redgrave, clerk in the office of the Commissioner of woods and forests; Mr.H.J.Hewlett, keeper of the land Revenue records; and Mr.John.Clutton, receiver of land revenues for the Crown in the County of Suffolk, spoke to the purchase of lands from the Crown by the Great Eastern Railway Company, to the Company being licensed to take shingle, and to the negotiations with the company for further land which the Company required. Mr.Robert William Hook, Ex-Coxswain of the Lowestoft Lifeboat, stated that the whole of the beach above ordinary high-water mark, at Lowestoft, lying along the North-East side of the harbour, and out of which the new dock was in course of excavation, had been formed by the accumulation of land and shingle caused by the Lowestoft harbour works. The advance of the beach and the receding of the high-water mark could be plainly perceived from time to time. It was not observable in calm water, but at other times the progress of the beach was visible from month to month, and when the wind was in certain quarter and the tide high, from day to day. Many thousands of tons of sand and shingle have been taken for ballast, and but for that advance would be much more rapid. A wreck upon the coast some 16 or 17 years ago caused a rapid increase of beach. Mr.J.B.Swan, Gat pilot, of Lowestoft; Mr. Benjamin. Taylor, master fisherman, of Lowestoft; Mr.Ward, retired ship chandler, of Lowestoft; and the Harbour master, gave similar evidence. At the conclusion of the arguments, which were very lengthy and of exceedingly technical character, their Lordships reserved judgement.

From January 1st, 1887 Robert had a series of letters published under his pseudonym pen-name of "An Old Salt". Inefficient Lifeboat, speaking with all the experience of a practical seaman, and his communication is consequently one of National Importance. With the blunt directness which characterizes the statement of his class, "An "Old Salt" asserts that the members of the Aldeburgh Lifeboat crew" have lost faith" in their boat," and says that the Aldeburgh men "openly express a desire" for a boat of "the old-fashioned model". He went on to further state that in the opinion of practical men no "self-righting" Lifeboat could have lived in the sea and under the conditions which prevailed when the Southwold boat went to the rescue of the shipwrecked crews off Thorpeness the previous Monday morning. (referring to three vessels which struck the sands and the crews were rescued from the riggings). Not only is this statement supported by the ordinary practical knowledge possessed by seafaring men, but it is also based upon local experience which renders it peculiarly forcible. Since 1809 the Lifeboat crews of Lowestoft and Pakefield have saved more than 700 lives without an accident, and we have no right to assume that the bravery of our east-coast seamen has in any way diminished, or that they are any less ready to go to the rescue of imperilled crews now than they have been during the last eighty years. The fact that the Aldeburgh Lifeboat crew has not sufficient confidence in its boat to venture out in her in such weather as that of Monday morning-knowing as we do that the Aldeburgh crew is "Always ready"-shows to our mind that there is something highly unsatisfactory in the character and qualities of the self-righting boats of the National Lifeboat Institution. Whether the Aldeburgh men are right or wrong in their view of this matter is a point which should certainly be cleared up, and we would specially invite the earnest attention of the Institution to the pertiment facts set forth in the letter of "An Old Salt". He went on to state; Whilst English seamen are ready at all times to risk their own lives in attempting to save the lives of others, it is but right that every effort should be made to provide the rescuers with boats upon which they can place the most complete reliance, -yours. An Old Salt.

Letter to the editor, The Lifeboat Question, Wednesday 2nd March 1887. Sir, -Colonel. Leathes is a most determined champion of our local type of Lifeboat, and I hope some good may come of his keeping the matter before the public. The letter from Mr.Teedale accompanying that of the gallant colonel, coming from such a veteran, speaks for itself.

Mr.Teedale, of Yarmouth, has designed and built Lifeboats and beach yawls for the last fifty years, and has always been an enthusiast for experiments with models. This gentleman built the celebrated Royal Victoria Beach yawl that challenged a celebrated American schooner a few years since, to sail for a large sum of money from one day to six in any weather, and from any place, but the yankee was affaid to accept the challenge and refused to enter into the contest, our east coast boats so famous for their speed. I give this as an instance of this gentleman's skill. I am prejudiced against the self-righting boats, as I saw one upset and drown and injure several crew, a personal friend being one of the number drowned, who had gone off as a volunteer. I think with Mr.Teedale that the water has too much play in the well of the boat, and it would be better for a partition to run fore and aft and also one amidships, as the motions of the boat, in my opinion, would be much easier. The last new improved self-righters have had very heavy keels put in, and everything done to get stability, but there has been no alteration of model. Hence the results in the latest disaster involving a self-righter. The method of testing our Lowestoft Lifeboat was to launch in the face of a gale, sail over the breakers on the sands, then tack into the middle of them, lower sail and let her drive to leeward, the boat being most of this time broadside, and this is repeated, the boat being placed in every possible position to test her. This is a proper and practical test, far different from that carried out in a dock, by the builders of the self-righters. I quite agree with the Colonel that theirs is not a fair test of their requirements. The reason of the extra cost of the self-righting boats is the splendid work put into the boat by the builders, and though bad in principal and in model, they are about the best built and fitted boats I ever saw, no expense or time being spared to give them a finish. This is all good as far as it goes, but utility and safety are the things required. My father has a testimonial for life-saving services in the Lowestoft Lifeboat, when the crews of two vessels were saved (18 men) during a heavy gale. I have all my life been connected with the Lifeboat and beach-men. – I am An Old Salt.

On Friday 29th July 1887, Robert Hook who was walking on the beach near Lowestoft's Ness-point, discovered some clothes and on searching he found a vistors card in a pocket bearing the following name and address: - Joseph. Richard. Dursee, 46, South-street, Greenwich, S.E. The newspapers at the time reported that Dursee had been lodging at Lowestoft, and was fond of swimming, and it was feared he had been carried away with the currents, which Hook said ran very strongly at this point. The body was never recovered.

Letter to the editor, Tuesday 10th January 1888. Sir, -The Royal National Lifeboat Institution has just issued a report of its doings during the past year, the twelve months having passed without an accident. Three hundred and sixty-eight lives have been saved, and ten ships were helped into ports by the Lifeboats, and the boatmen also put off 89 times in reply to signals of distress, to find their services were not required. This brings up the total saved by the society since its formation in 1824 to 33,243 lives-a truly splendid record, of which us in Lowestoft can lay claim to 700 of that total, of which we may well feel proud. The Institution also gave rewards to the crews of shore boats, and others for the saving of 204 lives during the year. The committee of the Institution are making an urgent appeal for funds to replace a large number of the 291 boats by others with all the latest improvements, such as water ballast, and centre keels. I have read the reports of the new boats lately launched, and find that self-righting is still the principal object aimed at. The model, however, remains the same, and it is still to be demonstrated whether the new boats are superior to the old. Their sailing qualities to windward will not be improved till the air cases fore and aft are discontinued. With so much surface to the wind and sea a boat will never do so well under sail. The great thing, in my opinion,it is to get a boat that will not upset. Our east coast boats are so snug in the water; and with the water ballast inside and the large cork belt outside they are as nearly as possible uncapsizable. The self-righting boats are very lively in a sea, way on top of everything. Our boats go through the sea, and will carry a heavy press of sail. The speed they get in broken water is "a treat." Sometimes very little of the boat is seen; the men hold on by the ridge ropes. The Caister Lifeboat men often have to cross three sand banks before approaching a wreck, the boat being sailed to the utmost-as long as sails and spars will stand it-which could not be done with self-righters, the speed of which is very small. To obtain the righting power, most of the benefical elements of a Lifeboat are sacrificed.

The self-righting boats have been in use nearly 80 years. The records of the Lowestoft, Pakefield and Caistor boats will compare favourable with any others on the coast. Not a single accident has ever occurred at either of these places. We have had a dozen boats, large and small, and in no cases, have accidents occurred with our boats. Various little improvements have been made in our boats, but the principle remains the same, and we are quite satisfied that it is the right one. The boats having gone through the several tests, us beach-men say, "Give us a boat that will keep the right side uppermost, and not a toppler." The Caister boat once rescued a crew on the Cross Sands, having her bow stove in, and then sailed back over three sand-banks- about ten miles-all landing safe. I must just say a word about shore-boats. At one time many lives were saved by the beach yawls. The rivalries between the companies at Lowestoft caused fearful risks to run, but it was these contests that brought out the splendid qualities of the men and trained up a class of daring fellows-an honour to the nation-of whom we, in this district, should be justly proud. There are 16 boats on the Teesdale principle belonging in the Royal. National. Lifeboat. Institution, and four volunteer boats of the same build. I witnessed the design of a Norfolk and Suffolk boat take the first prize at the great Fisheries Exhibition in London in 1883, being exhibited by Mr.Critten, of Yarmouth, in competition with a number of others. The contrast between the Self-Righters and our own boat is very great, when there placed together, as I have seen them at Lowestoft and Harwich, and the remarks of our men are not very complimentary respecting the "topplers." I will say, in conclusion, that the institution will be very glad of assistance by means of funds, to place new boats and give rewards for services to the gallant fellows who man them. I am An Old Salt.

Roberts letter to the Journal in Saturday 4th February 1888 edition. The Lifeboat Question. Sir, - I have been away from home, or should have noticed your Sizewell correspondent's letter earlier. I quite endorse Mr.Woolfield's remark's, that the only competent men to judge of the requirements of a Lifeboat are the beach-men who work them. Naval men, as a rule, are bad boatmen, and know little of handling of boats in a seaway. The beach-men have been brought up to the work, and know what is required. The superiority of the sunk boats was fully demonstrated at Sizewell on December 26th, 1886 when comparisons, very unfavourable to the Aldeburgh and Thorpe boats, were made while the Southwold boat was much admired by the Aldeburgh men. The Thorpe boat was in Lowestoft last autumn, and was the subject of some very disparaging remarks by our beach-men. The good qualities of a Lifeboat have been sacrificed to obtain the righting power. Most of us have heard of the Bradford- the Ramsgate Lifeboat- but I would ask has her self-righting power been any benefit to her? And could she not have done quite as well or better without it? Mr.Woolfield says it is all now up to the Royal.National.Lifeboat.Institute,but I think it is not too late to induce the beachmen of Aldeburgh, Thorpe, and Dunwich, to get one of Mr.Critten's exhibition boats, and if

Mr.Woolfield could help them to do so, that would be something like a real friend, as he undoubtably is. I have always been an admirer of the Lifeboat and the Yawl, Ive enjoyed sailing both. I may also remark that I admire the R.N.L.I, and consider it one of the grandest and most-noble in the world, as well as the officers and men that man her Majesty's ships, who are second to none for pluck and skill. An Old Salt.

On Tuesday 24th June 1890, in court was Robert and the Old Company along with the Great Eastern Railway Company, the former being owners of the yawl Success, and the gig Jenny Lind, and the latter the steam-tugs, Rainbow and Despatch. Both claimed for salvage services rendered to the Londonderry steamship "Barmston" in the North Sea. Their case was that about noon on the 14th March information was received at Lowestoft that a ship was ashore on the Holm Sand, and a number of Old Company members went out to her. She proved to be the steamship "Barmston," of Sunderland, laden with coals. The tug Despatch came up, and was at once engaged, with the beachmen of whom there were 65, to get the Barnston off and tow her into Lowestoft harbour. The beachmen jettisoned the cargo, and the Despatch towed ahead for half an hour without success. Subsequently the tug Rainbow and Imperial also came out from Lowestoft and were likewise engaged to tow ahead. The Barmston was got off the next day, and was towed to a safe anchorage in the North Roads. The defendants admitted the service, but contended that the Barnston was never in any danger. The Court awarded plantiffs £600, with costs.

The photo below was taken in 1892 by Mr.Broughton, and started a relationship in which he took some of the best and only know photos of my cousin which went on to be published in newspapers, books and postcards at the time. These photos are so rare to find that Ebay and the Lowestoft Heritage centre where the only places to find these images.

This photo over the page was taken just days after Robert received his "Osip" awards, which included a pair of engraved binoculars given to him at the town hall, but these binoculars were engraved "To Robert William Hook, coxswain of the Lowestoft lifeboat Laetitia, from the Imperial and Royal Austrian Government in recognition of the valuable service rendered to the crew of the Austrian brig OSIP on the 13th January 1866". But at the time the lifeboat was the Victoria, which was not replaced with the Laetitia until early 1869, Robert didn't say anything at the time about the inscription mistake as he was just happy to get a new pair of binoculars.

Photo by   Boughton.

Robert Hook.

On September 7th, 1892, twenty-six years after Hook and his crew rescued the crew of the Austrian brig Osip, they were rewarded, the delay was down to the fact that at the time when details had been forwarded to the Austrian government, the country was at war with both Prussia and Italy and the matter was put on one side. The appearance of Mr. R. W. Hook, and his comrades (D. Cook, E. Ellis, etc), several of them arrayed in the cumbrous cork life-jackets in which they proceeded to the now famous wreck, as they marched up to and took seats at the table in front of the chairman, evoked loud applause from the assembly.

Lowestoft's Mayor Mr. B. M. Bradbeer, distributed awards to the coxswain and surviving members of the crew. Robert Hook was presented with a pair of binoculars and three guineas, remarking that he hoped he would make good use of them. The crew was given one guinea each, for each time that they had gone out. If in the meantime a crew member had died his remaining family was given the money. The awards were as follows; - Samuel Mewse, James Yallop., an aged looking man and lame, Richard Butcher's eldest son, the widow of Alfred Mewse, the widow of James Ayers, the widow of George Yallop, the daughter of William Rose, the widow of Charles Liffen, the widow of William Capps, the son of John Gurney, the widow of Benjamin Butcher, the grandson of William Gallant, W. Norman, senior., W. Norman, Junior., the representative of James Cook, James Clarke, John Mewse, Thomas Rose, G. Allerton, Edward Ellis, W. S. Barnard, W. Spurgeon, James Yallop, senior., (a very aged man), George Clarke and William Ayers. One of the crew was dead, named Mewse, it was stated he had not left a widow. As the various recipients, male and female, stepped forward to receive the money awarded them they were loudly cheered by the large audience, who, evidently, keenly relished the scene. Several of those entitled were not present. E. Ellis left before the presentation.

At the time David Cook, one of the crew, declined to take the sum of one guinea tendered to him by the Mayor. Cook's refusal was grounded on a strong sense of injustice, as it was notorious he was in the Lifeboat on both occasions, although by some inexplicable blundering on the part of someone, he was only reported to the Austrian Government as having been to the wreck once. Mr. Foster, who was present at the distribution, and had, in fact, materially aided in securing the rewards, was disgusted with the paltry sum awarded, in the face of the Austrian Government's extraordinary eulogy of the heroism displayed by his constituents, Hook and his fellow band of gallant Lifeboat men. He at once publicly made himself responsible for the presentation the following year on August 22nd in the south pier pavilion, and further, wrote to the Austrian Government, stating in very plain terms his opinion of the meagreness of the reward. After several letters and interviews with the Austrian Ambassador and Consul-general on the subject he elicited that local magnates were really responsible for the small pecuniary awards. The Consul-General was, however, so struck with Cook's heroism that he gave another guinea out of his own pocket. Mr.Foster took the trouble to come over to Lowestoft, and visited the Beach in search of Cook, to whom he handed the well-earned money in the presence of "Bob" Hook and several other lifeboat veterans "All of the olden time." The following year Mr. Foster gave each of the remaining crew a silver medal, the remaining crew were as follows; Robert William Hook, Samuel Mewse, David Cook, George Yallop, Robert James Yallop, Richard Butcher, Alfred Mewse, James Ayers, Joseph Swan, John Mewse, William Gallant, James Clarke, William Norman, William Norman Jr, William Burwood Capps, William Capps, Charles Liffen, Thomas S Rose, John Gurney, William Swan, William Rose,

Edward Ellis, William Spurgeon, Charles Allerton, George Clarke, Samuel Taylor, Benjamin Butcher, William Ayers and lastly William Smith.

The Crew of *Laetitea*
Better late than never

The inscription on the reverse of this medal says presented to each member of the crew of the Lowestoft lifeboat *Laetitia* for the gallant rescue of seven Austrian sailors from the brig *Osip* lost off Lowestoft during the storm of 13 January 1866 'Esto Perpetua'.

At the time of the rescue the lifeboat was named *Victoria*, details of the rescue were overlooked by the Austrian government because of the Austro-Prussian War, 1866.

Twenty-six years later these privately made medals were presented to the crew of the *Victoria*, renamed *Laetitia* in 1869.

J Mewse

On Friday 6th July 1894, a thunderstorm of extreme power broke over the east coast, heavy torrents of rain fell, and the lighting was intense. Sadly, two men lost their lives at sea. They were part of the crew of the "Jenny Lind", a Lowestoft fishing boat, which was fishing about seven to eight miles out at sea. The boat was riding out the worst of the storm, and at 2 a.m., on Saturday morning was then returning to Lowestoft when the vessel was struck by Lighting. Samuel J.Turrell, the skipper, was at the tiller, he was knocked to the deck but not hurt; Samuel Mewse and Charles Ellis, who were also on deck, were killed instantaneously, while John Burgess was knocked unconscious. The funeral of Samuel Mewse and Charles Ellis, Longshoremen took place on the following Tuesday afternoon at the cemetery, in the presence of a large assemblage. The two coffins, covered with wreaths, were borne into the beach village church from the hearse's by twelve stalwart Lifeboat-men, including coxswain W.Capps, followed by the widows and numerous relatives, the rear being brought up by a number of Lifeboat veterans and beach company colleague's, headed by the renowned "Bob Hook", ex-coxswain of the lifeboat in which the deceased had often gone out, it had only been a couple of years past that Samuel had been recognized for his part in the "osip" rescue. The officiating clergyman was the rev. D.Dickson, vicar of Christchurch. The two graves were dug side by side, and while the committal portion of the burial service was being said, many of the vast congregation were moved to tears. Prior to pronouncing the benediction, the vicar addressed a few earnest words to those assembled. The floral tributes included a couple of beautiful anchors of flowers sent by the Old Company of beach-men, of which the deceased were members. Ellis left a widow and four young children, while Mewse left a widow who was disabled, the Old Company did their bit in providing for their needs.

In July 1894 Robert wrote and had a letter published under his pseudonym pen-name of "An Old Salt". "Old Salt" writes: - "There have been several yawls built at Lowestoft before "Georgiania", was built for the Young Company, and all for the Old Company. First was the South End Friends, a large yawl that saved several crews from shipwreck. Next came the Greyhound, a boat noted for going to windward. She was very sharp and fast and certainly lived up to her name. The Old Company had four yawls alone which carried the name Happy New Year, others being Princess Royal, Beeswing, Bittern and Mosquito. The Mosquito was the first to have two sails, since then all the boats carried them, a jib being used at regattas. It is doubtful if the speed of the boats is improved by the discontinuance of the main sail. In the early days most of the yawls were fully tarred but in later years as marine paints got better they were painted white with red or blue bottoms and with most Old Company boats, they had flags painted on the bow.

In 1896 Robert wrote again into the Local paper under his pen name and said that this year saw the end of most beach companies around the coasts as the decreasing fleets of brigs, Schooners made way for the steam cargo ship. The beach companies were fast losing their reputation and occupation, only fifty years ago, when an adverse breeze filled the coastline roadsteads with scores and hundreds of wind- bound vessels, the beachmen was so active and it was a profitable calling. Then, the gigs and yawls that then for weeks and months stood idle on the sands and boat sheds, were in constance use, and the crews that manned them had the greater part of the lifesaving and salvage work of the coast in their hands.

The above photo shows the Lowestoft Lifeboat Crew from 1892 posing alongside the "Samuel Plimsol", up to this point the crew used the boat "Stock Exchange" which was donated by the London stock exchange hence its name, but due to the fact that the crew didn't like the way she reacted when at sail she was rejected by them in favor for the Samuel Plimsol. It was said that due to the fame of the Plimsol that when she was retired she was cut into pieces and sold as souvenirs to local visitors to the town. The local paper at the time of this photo being published said that two famous coxswains were pictured, namely Jack Swan, who is remembered for the rescue of 25 crew of the "Hopeland" and the boat "Black Cat" and Robert Hook, but I'm not sure as it looks like his brother William. The names of the crew are: - Back row: Fred Jarvis, Robert Ridley Ayers, Ted Harmer, and Jack Swan (Crusty.") Second row: Joseph swan, Sam Turrell ("Slum"), Unknown, Tom Rose, Robert Saunders, Watcher Turrell, William Hook, John Mewse ("Crorney") Jack Rose (Jack Mike). Sitting: "Bosser" Ayers and Charlie Allerton.

In the September 7th, 1901 edition of the Black and White
Budget publication the above picture was printed. In spite of

the fact that the majority of visitors to Lowestoft frequented the southern end of the town, the north beach itself was not altogether devoid of interest, for it was in this quarter that the fishing element inhabited. Next to the Low Light the most conspicuous building on this portion of the beach may, perhaps, be considered the quaint old wooden structure shown in the previous picture. This building was the headquarters of the Old Company of Lowestoft beach-men, and was in existence for over a century till it was pulled down at the end of the Second World War due to shell damage. Adorning the exterior were several figure-heads and name-boards of vessels which had been wrecked off Lowestoft and to who's rescue the beach-men have had gone at various times in the course of their long career. Some of the old boys shown in the foreground of the picture had been members of the Old Company from their boyhood, and many are the tales of hardships which the old veterans recounted to visitors, as having been both witnessed and endured by them in their hazardous yet noble work of lending timely aid to "those in peril on the sea." Robert can be seen 5th from the left.

This is how the site of the Old Company shed looks today, a
waste ground near Ness point, it's such a shame back in the
40's nobody had the foresight on what Lowestoft needs now
and that's tourist's and if it was still there it would be an
asset to our maritime history. It would also be good if
someone had saved the figure heads and name boards from
the fire and their hiding in someone's garden shed just
waiting to be discovered.

In the next picture you can clearly see the front of the Old Company Shed, a copy of this picture can be found in the Lowestoft Maritime museum and it says from left to right the men are; Peter Smith- Tim 'brock' Ellis- William 'sheppey' Hook- Harris Allerton- John 'painter' Swan- Dixon Peek (seated).

In February 1932 long after roberts death and all the members in the picture the Lowestoft Sea Scouts adopted as their headquarters the most easterly situated building in the British Isles, and one of the most picturesque. They were to share with the Old Company of Lowestoft Beachmen, the associations of the old shed were sure to have impressed the scouts who used it.

In 1902 Mr.W.Boughton approached Robert and asked would he and the members of the company like to sit for a photo shoot for photographs to be made up into postcards, Robert and fellow members agreed and the photographs are a moment in time captured in black and white, these brave men at rest and play. The first photo captures three of the company playing nap and passing time on an unprofitable calm day in the rear of the Old Company boat shed, surrounded by the trappings of their job, namely sails and tackle. Robert's brother William is on the far right smoking his pipe, by the smile on his face he may-be holding a good hand.

"A Game of Nap" in the Most easterly House in England.

At around the same time Robert took his part in the Lowestoft carnival parade confirming his life time commitment to the lifeboat.

The second photo taken at the same time is Robert sitting outside the Old Company shed on the North beach on lookout duty with his telescope, I like the detail in the door above Roberts head of a spy hole hatch.

Lowestoft Fishing Industry — Lifeboat Hero.

In 1906 a letter was published in the Lowestoft Journal and is as follows; Bob Hook, an old and brave life-saving veteran. For thirty years and over he was coxswain of the Lowestoft lifeboat, and in that capacity he has the splendid record of having saved over six hundred lives, he has a silver medal for saving the crew of the Austrian brig Osip, one for the services rendered to the Berthon, a wreck so vividly described in a letter from Alderman Jefferies in the Lowestoft Journal last week and another for the Expedite, this later with the second class clasp from the RNLI, Bob Hook is now 79 years, bent and bowed and face forrowed and scarred by exposure to the lashing waves of the storm tossed North sea. It is thought, and rightly too, that some recognition should be made of his service by the town, so that in his old age he may-be heartened and brightened up. Alderman Jefferies has also made a suggestion in this direction.

In 1910 Robert was asked by a longtime friend would he mind in putting his reputation as Ex-Coxswain into supporting his campaign to be elected in the borough of Lowestoft, the friend was Harry Foster.

BOB HOOK

(Ex COXSWAIN LOWESTOFT LIFEBOAT),

SAYS:—

"Vote for Foste

THE TRUE FRIEND OF ALL

LOWESTOFT FISHERMEN."

Printed and Published by Flood & Son, Ltd., The Borough Press, Lowestoft.

At the time of asking Robert wasn't feeling 100%, but didn't want to let down his good friend and longtime supporter Harry just because of his own fragility, so he pulled out a chair from his dining room, put it on the cobbles in the back garden and sat for the electioneering card photo wearing his medals. Harry Foster won the General Election that year with a total of 6530 votes, beating the other candidate Mr. E. Beauchamp's total of 6294 by a majority of just 236 votes.

Taken in 1910 by Thomas Boughton this photograph shows four members of the Old Company who served together as Lowestoft Lifeboat Crew members whose combined ages totalled 312 years. Left to right- Bob Hook (75). Mathew Coleman (81), John Colman (80) and James Burwood (76). This picture was deemed so good technically that it was awarded a Gold medal in the Berlin international exhibition.

You can see in the back ground several name boards from wrecked ships salvaged by the Company including the "Agathe Scheibert" which on Christmas Eve 1869 wrecked off Lowestoft and eleven crew were saved. If you notice this picture is taken at a right angle to the previous photo of the three old boys playing Nap ten years before, you can see that John Coleman has aged 10 years and he is still wearing the same hat!

MR. ROBERT HOOK,
COXSWAIN OF THE LOWESTOFT LIFEBOATS
FOR 30 YEARS.

Chapter Five

The Heroes of the Holm and Newcome Sands

In 1892 the Lowestoft Journal ran a story on Robert as he reminisced on his thirty-year service and is as follows.

Of late the Deal boatmen have had their daring brought prominently before the public. Our own gallant beach-men, whose life-saving exploits are not one with less brilliant, have somehow been relegated to the cold shade of obscurity. An old proverb has it that familiarity breed's contempt, and, possibly, constant familiarity with these unassuming local heroes may be responsible, if not exactly for contempt, at lease for the indifference with which their claims to national recognition have hitherto been passed over by their own townsmen. Yet another ancient adage alleges that no prophet is of any account in his own country; and here we have, in all probability, the gist of the whole matter in a nutshell. Distance lends enchantment to the view and frail human nature will ever be investing objects from afar with idealistic splendour, which at home it's treated as almost unworthy of consideration. Like the modest violet fated to bloom unseen, and waste its sweetness on the desert air, the heroic Lowestoft beach-men has been content to save lives and not to trouble himself about the trumpeting forth of his fame. The Lowestoft Beach population are in every sense of the term a peculiar people. From earliest childhood inured to hardship and contention with the cruel sea, which they regard as their natural enemy; the merciless devourer of their kindred, the pitiless propagation of wailing widows and orphans, they acquire a sturdy independence of character unknown to the denizen of the inland town. They have inter-married for generations amongst their own particular class, and there are few Beach families we believe which are not, like the Highland clan of yore, connected by marriage, or some claim slight or strong of kinship. They also evidently consider that sufficient unto the day is the evil thereof, and takes small concern for the morrow. Till excited by a prospective wreck, or engaged in wrestling their harvest from the silvery hosts of the Northern Sea, they are, generally speaking a quiet, unobtrusive class of persons; but when the latent Viking spirit is roused in their breasts, they are like the ocean in a storm. Before lifeboats were thought of they wrestled with the hungry deep, and dragged its palpitating prey from its fury by means of their historic "yawls," or "yolls" and gigs. The gigs are long light boats constructed to combine swiftness with strength, and are employed to carry assistance to vessels on the sands or in distress, and when manned and double banked it is amazing at what rate they are propelled. Their very swiftness, on the principle of whirling a full glass round without spilling the water in it owing to the rapidity of the motion, prevents the sea from swamping them. The yawls are capacious boats of larger and stronger build than the gigs; they are fitted with foresail and mizen, and are used in rough weather for the same purpose as the gig is used in fair weather. In days gone by with these gigs and yawls our handy beach-men performed marvellous life-saving feats, which the lifeboats of today, with all their improvements cannot surpass, if they can equal. Before the doomed ship was among the breakers, which were to prove her tomb, the keen-sighted detected the inevitable; their boats were immediately launched and away on their life saving errand. Often fierce was the contest among them, frequently ending in blows, for a seat of honour in the yawl proceeding on some apparently forlorn hope to a sinking ship barely discernible above the angry crests of the waves.

Three wet shirts in a day was no uncommon experience of these gallant East Coast heroes. As that grand old beach-man "Bob" Hook says, "When we went, we went, and we always

211

got what we went for." And the reward for thus carrying their lives in their hands to save men from watery graves, too often the magnificent sum of ONE SHILLING. For the beach community, it was ruled by unalterable law of co-operation, whereby all who lend the slightest aid in getting the boat off and hauling them up shared equally with those who braved death to rescue the ship wrecked ones. The Deal and Ramsgate boatmen had a good friend in Sir Moses Montefiore, the late benevolent Hebrew centenarian. When they went off to a wreck, Sir Moses arranged so that on their return they were regaled with a hot repast. And richly they deserved it. But Lowestoft beach-men have had no Sir Moses Montefiore to evince such truly practical benevolence in their behalf or sing their praises. We are informed Deal boatmen now among us admit that they have no such seas as Lowestoft beach-men are used to. They had no idea till they came to Lowestoft that the seas were so heavy in the locality. And here we wish it to clearly under-stood that in our attempt this week to direct attention to the gallantry of Lowestoft beach-men, we do not intend for one moment to depreciate the noble careers of the "Heroes of the Goodwin Sands." On the contrary, we appreciate to the upmost-no one more so-their undoubted heroism.

In illustrating the claims of the Lowestoft beach-men to position in the van of the Noble Army of Life-Saving Heroes, we have selected incidents in the career of "Bob" Hook, as he is affectionately called by those who have been associated with him for years in his dangerous vocation of coxswain of the local lifeboat. Robert William Hook is 64 years of age, a giant 6ft.3in., in height. In his prime he must have possessed the strength of a Hercules. From the early age of 16 till he retired from the coxswain-ship of the lifeboat a few years ago, he was engaged in saving life from wrecks by the aid of yawls, gigs and lifeboats, and has aided in rescuing from watery graves very nearly 600 persons. For 30 years he was coxswain of the various lifeboats stationed at Lowestoft. We interviewed "Bob," but found him, like most genuine heroes, unwilling to talk about his exploits, and treating the most thrilling episodes in his career as if of the ordinary complexion. One thing he was most anxious to impress on us, was, that better men than he had with him in the lifeboat he commanded could not be found at Deal or anywhere else. He was never weary of repeating that England might justly be proud of the lifeboat crews furnished from the ranks of the Lowestoft beach-men. A brave companion named "Ben Taylor," 76 years of age, who had accompanied him on many of his life-saving expeditions, the very opposite of "Bob" in height, was with him during our interview, and from time to time interpolated interesting scraps of information. We have preferred to give Mr. Hook's own accounts of a few of the typical "jobs" in which he and his gallant crews have been engaged, in the order in which we "wormed" them from his reluctant lips. They are not chronologically arranged, but any -one can easily test their accuracy by consulting the lifeboat records on the shed on the beach or by inquiry among his neighbours. As "Bob" laughingly remarked, "I've an awful bad head for dated." "Ben" Taylor on the contrary, seemed to possess a head for dates. One word before proceeding further, can the Lifeboat authority inform us why no Lowestoft man has been selected as a coxswain judge on the trials. Doubtless the Institution has some good reason for the omission, and apparent slighting of the claims of Lowestoft lifeboat experts, but the matter has been rather freely commented on, as it is alleged that one of the selected coxswain judges has had only a very few years practical experience.

But back to our story. On the 21st December 1847, a vessel was observed to have been driven by the wintry gale clean over the Holm Sand, Hook and some brave companions at once put off in the yawl Princess Royal to know whether the vessel required assistance. They were told no assistance was required then, the vessel came into the Roads and brought up. The next day Hook and his mates put off in the gig Salem to repeat their offer of assistance, which again was declined. Coming from the vessel those in the gig sighted a Dutch galliot on the Holm Sand, full of water, and met the wind blowing very hard from the east. They at once rowed out on the sand and spoke to the crew of a Revenue cutter's gig which was lying a breast of the sinking vessel. The Revenue men enquired whether Hook and his mates thought about going to the vessel. Hook replied," We don't know." The Revenue men said," There's too much sea for you; we daren't go!" At this time the cutter signalled for the gig to return, which they did. In the meantime, four people could be seen clinging to the mast of the sinking Dutchman, and regardless of the danger to themselves Hook and his comrades rowed through heavy surf and sea, and rescued every man. There was so much sea that the crew were filled nearly up to their throats with water. Such was the dangerous position of the gig that the crew had to back her out of the breakers they dare not turn her. Having rescued the Dutchman, the Salem went alongside the Revenue cutter, the commander of which gave them some grog, as the weather was so bitterly cold. Shortly after the crew was rescued the galliot went to pieces.

The third night after this gallant exploit a brig called the Hearts of Oak went aground on the Newcome Sands, and immediately filled with water. Hook and his comrades, notwithstanding the fearful weather and the bitter cold, put out in their boat, and rescued the crew of six men, landing them safely at Lowestoft. For saving 10 men from watery graves at the risk of their own lives Hook and his crew received the munificent reward of 1 shilling each. This is how England always rewards her genuine heroes.

During a heavy gale of wind a few months later on, the "Mary Young", a large North Country barque, bound for Genoa, struck on the Newcome and knocked her rudder to pieces. At that time such was the violence of the gale no less than 13 other vessels were riding in the Roads with the "unions down" as signals of distress. Hook, and his gallant crew of Lowestoft beachmen, immediately put out to the Mary Young's assistance, and rescued some 10 or 12 men at the utmost peril of their lives. As Hook dryly remarked, "We hant no steam tugs" "them to tow us out and in". When we got ashore with the rescued crew we couldn't get out again. If we could have got out, we should have got all off."

It was blowing a hurricane from the S.W., when about 10 o'clock in the morning of the 1st November 1859, the steamer Shamrock was discovered coming for the Holm Sand. Hook and his merry men at once launched their lifeboat, the dearly-beloved Laetitia, and proceeded to her assistance. On reaching her they found that the crew fully realised their danger, and wanted to leave the steamer. The laetitia anchored, wore down to them, and hauled fourteen men from the wreck through the raging water. During this Hook lay with his lifeboat "full and full," and taking every sea on the broadside. The captain of the steamer was the last to leave, and having hauled him safely on board, the laetitia proceeded for the beach, where she safely landed her precious freight. This glorious act the Royal National Lifeboat Institution decided should be recorded in their minutes. They also resolved as follows: -" That the silver medal of the Royal National Lifeboat Institution be presented to Robert Hook for his general gallant services in the Lowestoft lifeboat, in rescuing life from shipwreck, and particularly for his exertions in the said lifeboat in aiding to save the crew of fourteen men of the steamer Shamrock, of Dublin, which was wrecked on Holm Sands on the 1st of November 1859."

In the same week, at about 7 o'clock in the dim November morning, the Lord Douglas, a scotch schooner, parted from her anchors and drove ashore on Corton Flat. She immediately filled with water, and Hook and his comrades, having been informed by a messenger from Corton on horseback of the disaster, got out their boat, and wore down in a heavy sea to rescue the crew. Five poor fellows were taken out of the schooner's foretop in a very exhausted condition, and one was so overcome that he fainted away. Having accomplished their life-saving errand and got their anchor, the lifeboat men were beating home when such was the violence of the gale that they split their canvas, and were compelled to run ashore near Corton Pole. In the afternoon of the same day the schooner Silver also parted from her anchor and drove on to Holm Sand. Although their sails were rendered useless by the disaster of the morning, Hook and his comrades were not to be daunted in their efforts to save life. Hook borrowed "yawl" sails from the North Road Company, and gallantly launched again, and in a tremendous heavy sea rescued four people from seemingly certain death.

At 3 o'clock one morning, when it was dark and thick with rain, the Corton people reported that the brig Queen of the Tyne was on her beam ends among "Golloping Tom," a name given to a speciality turbulent portion of "Corton Patch." Hook's lifeboat was immediately launched and proceeded to the brig's assistance, as they went through the heavy seas they could just observe a small speck, which turned out to be the brig in trouble. Hook let go his anchor thinking they had ebb tide enough to allow them to veer down to her, but it turned out that there was not tide enough. Having got their anchor, they reached in and tacked off till they got windward of the brig, and then "spooned" down before the wind to her. They called out to the crew of eight men huddled together on the maintop-gallant yard to keep their spirits up as they were coming to save them. As the brig heeled down into the roaring sea, Hook and his comrades lifted the crew one by one from the yard into the lifeboat. To show the danger to the lifeboat men who effected this gallant rescue, we may say that Hook himself was pulled out of the lifeboat into the sea by the brig's maintop gallant brace. Before the lifeboat reached the shore with the rescued crew, the brig had disappeared in the seething waves.

On the 13th of January 1866, a large Austrian brig, laden with maize, went aground on the north part of Holm Sand. The small yawl, the young Prince, belonging to the Young Company, pluckily went to her assistance. On getting alongside the brig, however, nobody got into the boat, and the crew of the yawl signalled for a bigger boat. The Albatross answered the signal. By the time the Albatross got to the brig, the wind and sea had increased so much that she dare not board her, but signalled for the lifeboat. The Laetitia was immediately launched and towed out by the tug Rainbow through such a heavy sea that the tug was continually in danger of filling her engine-room with water. The Laetitia was towed to windward outside of the Holm, and when the tug let go, the lifeboat set sail and got as near to the distressed vessel as possible and let go her anchor. The anchor, however, unfortunately came home, so Hook slipped the cable and went for the tug to tow them in for another cable. As an illustration of the terrible state of the weather just at this time, we may here mention that the ill-fated Gorleston lifeboat having put off to another brig's assistance, she was capsized and 13 of her brave crew met with the watery graves they were seeking to rescue others from. In the meantime, Hook signalled the Austrian brig which had parted from her anchor, where they could go ashore without taking much harm. Having been supplied with a new cable and another anchor, the laetitia returned on her mission of mercy to the brig. Just as they reached the vessel's deckhouse, to which the crew of 11 hands and the pilot had attached themselves for safety with lines, gave way, and every soul was submerged in the hissing sea. Hook and his crew managed to rescue several of the poor fellows, including the pilot, who, however, shortly afterwards died in the boat. Four of the crew where drowned, the laetitia being unable to render them any assistance. A memorial, setting forth the highly meritorious services rendered by Hook and his gallant comrades on this memorable occasion, was prepared and forwarded to the Austrian Government, but, strange to say, from that day to this nothing has ever been heard in reference to it. It may have miscarried. Perhaps it is not now too late to endeavour to see that those valuable services are suitably recognized.

About four o'clock one dark, dank November morning some 12 years since the Pet, a fishing dandy, the property of Mr.Wm.Breach, made signals of distress by burning her nets, bedding, etc, for flares. The Lowestoft lifeboat immediately proceeded to the Newcome Sand, and on arrival there found the pet on here broadside. The poor fellows, in their desperation, had got the "bowls" knotted together to put under their armpits to help them to float from the sinking vessel, over which heavy seas were flowing. Twenty minutes later and she would not have been seen. The lifeboat went right alongside her, so close that they hit the wreck in order to get the crew on board. Hook and his comrades, however, succeeded in rescuing the whole of the crew, consisting of ten or eleven hands, and landed them safely in Lowestoft.

At 9 o'clock one morning about a year after the saving of the Shamrock's crew, a French brig with a cargo of timber, went aground on the South Holm during a southerly gale. The lifeboat immediately went to the brig's assistance, and having let go their anchor wore down to her through a heavy sea and rescued all her crew.

Before daylight in November 1867 the Yarmouth schooner Medora got on to the deadly Newcome Sand. Hook and his comrades saw her and launched at once with a crew of 11 instead of 19 hands. The wind was blowing a gale from the N.E, and there was a mountainous sea on. Owing to the bad weather the schooner's captain had broken his leg. The crew got the boat out, and two men had managed to get their maimed captain into it, when a tremendous sea came and ran the boat down stern first, broke the rope, and in a twinkling drowned all three. The remaining two of the crew, the lifeboat, under manned as she was, was just in time to get off before the schooner went down. For this glorious bravery Hook and his heroic comrades secured a pecuniary acknowledgment from the Lifeboat Institution.

It was late one afternoon in the fatal month of November that the brig Glenora, of Scarborough, went aground on the Corton Patch. Hook and his men boarded her in a little "yoll" and inquired of the captain whether he would let them take him and his crew on shore. He replied, "No, my ship will knock Yarmouth Roads all to pieces." Hook said, "Well, we'll go ashore and get the lifeboat, as we daren't stop here with this small yawl. If the wind increases rather more than you expect, make us signals with flares." By the time Hook and his comrades reached the shore for the lifeboat, the wind as they had foreseen, began to blow very heavily, and the captain of the Glenora flared as arranged. The lifeboat was launched and made for the distressed brig. The anchor was let go, the boat bore down to the brig got alongside, and took all the crew, numbering eight souls, on board. Hook had heard the main mast of the brig crack, and warned the crew to leave her as quickly as possible. Next morning not a vestige of the brig was to be seen.

By a singular coincidence in December of the same year another Scarborough vessel, yolept the Forest Flower, from a Spanish port, with grass and lead ore, met her fate exactly on the spot where the Glenora went to pieces. Before daylight the barque made signals of distress, and as she was on the place of the wreck of the Glenora this made it very dangerous for the lifeboat. However, they let go their anchor, and got alongside of the Forest Flower. It was then blowing hard, with a heavy sea on, yet Hook and his comrades rescued 16 fellow-creatures from an untimely death, and landed them safely in Lowestoft.

Just about daybreak of November 13th, 1872, the Norwegian brig Expedite, of drobak, was discovered by those on the beach to be on North Holm Sands. There was then a gale blowing from the north-east. At first those who discovered the vessel were not sure whether there were any living persons on board. As it was made out that men were walking on the deck, the lifeboat was immediately launched and taken in tow by the tug. Hook steered down to windward of the wreck, took in the sails, let go the lifeboat's anchor, and bore down to her. In the meantime, such was the terrible rolling of the sea that one of the crew of the lifeboat named Harry Hall had his leg broken. "Lor,bor," said Hook when recounting the incident, "Lor,bor, the sea did roll and no mistake." The Gorleston lifeboat had also put out for the wreck, but found it necessary to anchor in the channel. They said that the heavy seas, at times, prevented them from seeing the masthead of the Lowestoft boat, and they couldn't have believed that they could have lived in such awful seas-regular rollers. The laetitia could not at first relieve herself fast enough of the tons of water pouring into her; but afterwards, as Ben Taylor put it, "she came up like a little lady." Not with standing this terrible state of affairs, Hook and his comrades rescued all the crew of the doomed brig, amounting to ten persons, slipped the lifeboat's cable, and were towed into Lowestoft Harbour by the tug. For this single Act of valour "Bob" secured the second service clasp of the

R.N.L.I.

On the morning of the 14th November 1882, at about 10 or 11 o'clock, the Norwegian barque Berthon was sighted running for the Holm Sand. The Samuel Plimsoll lifeboat was immediately launched, and, towed by the tug, proceeded for the spot. The wind was blowing a heavy gale, and one boat was lost. On approaching the Berthon the lifeboat let go anchor, bore down to her, and found the beds and pillows floating out of her stern, and all her decks out and her cargo lying right open. In spite of these fearful conditions of the vessel, Hook and his boatman rescued eight men from imminent watery graves, and 15 minutes afterwards the vessel disappeared from view.

One morning around the 1860's a piece of the wreck of a foreign vessel came ashore, and Hook and his comrades heard that a vessel was lost. They put to sea, and on Corton Patch saw another piece of wreck floating among the billows. On it were the captain of the vessel and three poor fellows of the crew. They were so exhausted when rescued by Hook that they said they could not possibly have held on another quarter of an hour. When referring to this almost miraculous rescue Hook said, "God took us in his hand and placed us so that those poor fellows could be saved."

 One November night the smack Olive, of Harwich, was discovered aground on the Corton Patch, and burning flares. The wind was blowing hard with a heavy sea on, when the lifeboat, manned by Hook and his comrades, put out to the smack and rescued 12 of the 15 hands, the Corton boat rescuing the other three. W.Capps, the present coxswain of the Lowestoft lifeboat, was then one of the crew of the Laetitia. When one of the poor fellows jumped from the Olive into the lifeboat, in a semi-nude state, his toe nail caught the face of Capps, who was waiting with extended arms to receive him, and tore furrows in it, him and his crew mates soon were landed in Lowestoft at 8.30 p.m. being taken to the Sailors Home.

On the 17th Jan 1869 the smack "Nautilus went aground that winters Sunday morning on the Corton Patch. The crew, consisting of four hands, their got into their little boat to leave the vessel. When, however, they saw the lifeboat with Hook on board, coming to the rescue they returned to the smack and boarded her on the starboard quarter. Just at that moment a tremendous sea broke, and catching the little boat, hove all but one of its occupants on to the vessel, and he hung on to the rail. The lifeboat crew sung out to know whether the hands were coming out of the smack, and their replying "Yes," the anchor was let go, the lifeboat got alongside of the wreck, the crew all jumped into her, and immediately they did so their vessel went down.

Just before the peep of 'day (day break) on the 17th of November 1862, the brig Louisa of Faversham got aground in an easterly gale on the Holm Sand. She quickly filled with water, and displayed signals of distress. The lifeboat was launched and proceeded to the brig's assistance, but on reaching the Holm the boat also grounded, and from 7 in the morning till 3 in the afternoon did Hook and his brave men lie in that perilous position, with seas breaking over them. They, however, succeeded in rescuing the crew of the brig, some nine or ten hands.

In the same week as the disaster to the Louisa, the ketch Union, of Portsmouth, laden with timber, grounded on the South Holm, and exhibited signals of distress. Hook, with his companions, launched a "yoll," and proceeded to the distressed ketch. There was, however, so much sea on that they thought it would be foolhardy to attempt to board the ketch. They were accordingly coming away to fetch their lifeboat, but Hook took his chance whereupon he immediately let go their anchor, got alongside the ketch, and safely took off her four crew.

On March 18th, 1873, during a strong gale from the North-east, the schooner Celine of Gravelines went on the Holm

Sands, Hook proceeded in a "yoll" to her assistance. The crew refused to leave the vessel because the captain would not. The Lowestoft men then left her, but the wind and sea increasing very much, they returned this time in the lifeboat. On again reaching the schooner the crew willingly got into the boat except the captain, who was drunk, and wouldn't budge an inch. The crew, five or six in number, were taken ashore, and again did Hook and his Lowestoft sea-braves return to the wreck, this time in the small lifeboat, because there was so little water on the sand. Notwithstanding the drunken captain swore that he would go to sleep with the ship, but the lifeboat men compelled him by force to be saved.

An Italian brig got ashore on the bar of the Stanford sometime around 1867, during very cold weather. There was a strong wind blowing, and the vessel quickly filled with water. The crew clambered into the rigging and the pilot on to the foreyard. Hook and his comrades put off to the wreck and rescued 10 out of the 14 crew. The pilot told the lifeboat men as they lifted him off the foreyard that he was afraid the Italians would stab him because he had lost the ship.

On a bitter cold December night in 1869, a brigantine called the Edina was lost on the Holm Sand. The bold and good laetitia, with Hook as coxswain, crossed the deadly sand, through fearful waves, to the rescue of the despairing crew. The hapless vessel as she lay on the sand was cruelly raked by tremendous seas. The crew, eight in number, were however, got off safely from the wreck into the lifeboat, which then victoriously scudded back home across the sands, the burial place of the vessel, which went to pieces before daylight.

At about 9 o'clock on a dirty night in January 1868, during a gale from eastward and a blinding fall of snow, the Roseberry, a strong brig from Sunderland, came ashore abreast of the Battery green. Hook and his comrades immediately launched a large punt from the beach, and, despite the deadly danger, reached the distressed vessel and rescued from the eagerly expectant clutches of Old Davy Jones, the despairing crew of 11 souls all told. The rocket lifesaving apparatus had been got ready for work, but before it could affect anything Hook and his men had forestalled it in its errand of mercy. Shortly after the rescue of the crew the Roseberry became a total wreck. That dirty January night was indeed an eventful one in Lowestoft Beach annals, for immediately after the wreck of the Roseberry a schooner, named the Rock Scorpion, went ashore on the South Beach. The rocket apparatus was on the scene, but, said Hook, "We meant for victory." The boat was quickly launched, and fiercely battling with the cruel surf, proceeded on her life-saving errand. The crew were at once rescued from their perilous position, all except the captain, who stubbornly refused to leave his disabled vessel. As, however, the ship was liable to break up at any moment, "Bob" Hook and "Dick" Butcher jumped aboard and compelled the skipper to be saved by throwing him into the boat, which, owing to the danger of the situation, was herself half full of water.

In 1867 the night before Christmas Eve night, during a gale from the eastward, and with the air thick with snow, news was brought that a large vessel was ashore on Lowestoft Point. Hook and his brave companions the neglected heroes of Lowestoft Beach, having manned a yoll, belonging to the North Roads Company, a yawl (called) the bonny "Moss Rose," pulled manfully to the wreck, and in terrific seas, known only in the locality of the Point of the Ness, rescued 10 poor benumbed fellow creatures from the yawning jaws of death. Just before the yawl reached the shore with the precious freight a heavy sea caught her on her broadside, and threw a portion of the crew out of her on to the beach. Some were a hundred yards to the south of her before they landed, providentially, unhurt.

The following night, Christmas Eve, was also a dreadful time. A perfect hurricane raged from the eastward, and rockets from the Corton Sand were seen, indicating that a ship was there in dire distress. The Laetitia lifeboat was immediately launched, and Hook and his noble crew proceeded to the sand, where they discovered a fine Norwegian three-mast schooner, in need of help. They dropped their anchor and veered down to her, the sea making a clean breach over the gallant Laetitia. Such was of the ill-fated vessel afterwards averred that they never saw the lifeboat till she suddenly appeared like a merciful apparition by their side. Eleven men snatched from destruction was the holy Christmas tide work of Hook and his brave comrades on this occasion.

And here it is but just, and it is the earnest request of Hook and his brave companions, that the gallant services of Captain Porter and Sterry, of the Harbour tugs, in connection with the glorious life-saving work of the laetitia and other boats, should be recognized. These noble men never flinch for an instant in towing the lifeboat through the greatest perils to the spot indicated for casting them off, and, we repeat, it is but just that in a record of the heroic deeds of Lowestoft Beach-men they should receive at least "honourable mention." Further we may say, we find that the statement with which we commenced these articles, on Hook's own modest computation, that he had aided in saving some 300 lives by means of lifeboat's "yolls," "gigs," etc is considerably within the mark. We learn that Hook's life-saving record is nearer 600 than 300 lives.

One more incident and we close our examples of East Coast heroism. At seven o'clock one January morning in 1872 or there-about's, the coastguard reported that an Ipswich schooner had been blown from her anchor and was aground near the pier where the crew, consisting of four men and a black boy, were in the most imminent danger of losing their lives. Immediately the affair was reported to "Bob," Hook he ran out of the Old Company shed, accompanied by three other daring spirits, and although it was blowing a heavy gale easterly he plunged into the sea and swam to the stranded vessel. There for three quarters of an hour he rendered all the assistance in his power, when he plunged overboard again, got his own punt out of the harbour returned to the vessel, rescued the crew, and landed them safely on the beach. His clothes, owing to the weather, were one sheet of ice. Our task is now done, but not from lack of materials, the foregoing being but the fringe of the heroic acts performed by our daring beach-men. We trust, however, that we have furnished sufficient evidence to prove that as lifeboatmen our local Toilers of the sea may justly claim the proud title of "SECOND TO NONE."

The picture above is a British 2-masted schooner, was spoken as a topmast schooner by beach-men.

Just before we concluded our interview with Robert he went over to a draw and pulled out a scrap book of newspaper cuttings and raised the issue of Superannuation of Lifeboat Veterans, and I think this letter from October 1892 say's it best on the issue: To the editor of the "Lowestoft Journal."

Dear Sir, - I see that attempts are being made in certain quarters to raise false issues and draw red herrings across the path in respect to your articles, etc., in reference to Lifeboat matters. Somebody has rushed into print and painted in glowing terms the so-called service of the Lifeboat a week or so ago, forgetful of how in really bad weather she was not allowed to venture forth to save unfortunate Lowestoft shrimpers from very serious danger. The gentleman referred to apparently suffering from cacoethes (an urge to do something inadvisable), infers that you have questioned the bravery of the Lowestoft beach-men. Now I have completely studied your articles, but have never seen anything in them in the slightest degree reflecting on the courage of the real old sea dogs who wouldn't think twice before plunging to the rescue of despairing drowning men. In fact the same individual a week or so ago was indignant because, as he alleged, you petted the Lowestoft beach-men and made too much of their heroism.

The issue that you have attempted to keep before the public

has always seemed to me to be a very plain one. A number of experienced lifeboat-men, who and whose ancestors had done excellent life-saving service, have been arbitrarily ordered by the Institution never again to enter the boats to endeavour to save life on pain of being prosecuted. These men naturally feel that a great slur is cast upon them, and complain that they have never been allowed to answer any charges made against them behind their backs. Gentlemen of position in the town and one hundred and fifty comrades on the beach have supported them in their appeal for ordinary English justice. You, realizing that the supply of men suitable to form crews of Lifeboats must by necessity always be precarious, owing to able bodied beach-man being called away on fishing expeditions, with the telegraph ship, etc, argue that five experienced men, who are on the spot, cannot with safety be arbitrarily excluded from proceeding to attempt to save life. You ask that the Lifeboat authorities will afford the men the means of publicly defending themselves against any influence which may have been brought to bear to secure the alleged unfair treatment to which they have been subjected. The Lifeboat authorities ignore the appeal of the men and all who back them; but so, they did in other cases, and as Hook, an ex-coxswain, at a public meeting once said, "Handcuffed" them so that disaster arose for which the innocent had to suffer. I am now back to London, and intend to extend the discussion of the question to the leading city papers, and bring the subject under the notice of the vast constituency from which the Lifeboat Institution draws its conscriptions. During my visit to Lowestoft I purposely associated with the tabooed men, and could find nothing of any account against them. I consider that you have only done your duty as a public journal in directing attention to the unsatisfactory state of affairs, and none but malignant enemies of the Lowestoft beach-men would attempt to obstruct your action. But I intended to write on the subject of the superannuation of wore out Lifeboat-men, who for a long series of years have braved every danger to health, life, and limb, till old age has laid them on the shelf crippled with rheumatism and unable to help themselves, although they have arrived at this pitiable condition through helping others. I say that the Institution ought to strain every nerve to raise a fund for superannuating such deserving subjects. I feel that if the matter were properly put before the public, and suitable guarantees given that the fund would not be abused by favouritism, no difficulty would be experienced in raising the sum required. I can assure you I do not intend to let the matter drop, and possibly as this and kindred Lifeboat subjects are being more widely discussed, we shall learn from other stations of complaints among the crews of the Institution boats. My letter must now be closed, and I beg to subscribe myself. Yours very faithfully, CIVITAS.

The Fishermans arms as it stands today in 2015, an empty plot.

Chapter Six

Death of a Hero

On June 30th, 1911 it was reported in the Lowestoft Journal

as follows, Robert. Hook, or, as everyone familiarly called him, Bob Hook, Lowestoft's great lifeboat hero, is dead. For months past the gnaried, weather beaten old sea warrior, of giant frame-he stood over 6ft.3ins-and once of immense strength, has laid helpless as a child, and on Wednesday afternoon the 28th of June he passed peacefully away. His death being in vivid contrast with the strenuousness of his young days, when he was coxswain of the lifeboat, and when, with lion-hearted courage, and never daunted when the call came to save life, as he said, "let the storm rage and the sea roar ever so fiercely".

Bob Hook's active days have long been over-he was 84 years of age and it has been somewhat of a reproach that an effort was not made to render his declining years more comfortable. He has been able to get along, for he was very thrifty, but it would have been an act of grace and an acknowledgement of his splendid service if there had been some recognition.

Bob Hook commenced his career as a lifeboat man when he was 16 years old, and for thirty years he was coxswain of the lifeboat. By means of the lifeboat, yawls and gigs, he helped to save the lives of 600 persons during his career. That career was, owing to unfortunate circumstances, which it would do no good to recount, ended some 30 years ago, Bob Hook ceased to be coxswain of the lifeboat. It was the general opinion at the time, and there are many now who express the view when the subject crops up, that Bob Hook was not to blame for what unfortunately happened that he was made a scapegoat for the sins of others.

To recount all the life-saving episodes in which Hook and his brave companions, the Lowestoft beach-men, had a share, would be a lengthy task, but one may be put forward in order to show the manner of man he was, duty first, and self-afterwards. Going back to 1847, when Hook was not quite 20, there was a brave rescue of the crew of a Dutchman that had been driven on the Holm Sand. Bob and his crew did not go in the lifeboat, but manned their gig, The Salem, and regardless of the heavy seas, they saved four men forming the crew of the Dutchman, the vessel going to pieces shortly afterwards. Much more might be said of Hook's life-saving feats, and they are legion, but enough has been presented to show that Robert never flinched when duty called, and that he was always "ready, aye, ready," when there were precious lives to be saved from a watery grave. It may be interesting to give names of some of those who fought the sea with Hook in the old days; Ben. Taylor, Alfred Mewse, Samuel Mews, John Mewse, Henry Norman, Samuel Turrell, Richard Butcher, William Smith, John Turrell, David Cook, Frank Smith, William Norman, William Rose, John Knights, Jas Yallop, Matthew Colman, John Linder, William Ayres, George Ayres, Edward Ellis, John Butcher, Jas Fletcher, Joseph Fletcher, William Armes, William Nobbs, James Hales, James Ayres, George Day, William Cooper, Charles Day, James Butcher, William Day, Harry Hall, William Capps, R Saunders, Jas Burwood and his brother William (Sheppy) Hook.

Some of these are still alive, and the death of their old comrade will undoubtedly lead them to talk over the daring deeds of bygone days. The funeral of the old sea hero takes place to-morrow (Saturday) afternoon.

The obsequies (funeral rites) were attended by thirty
lifeboatmen wearing their cork jackets, and eight of their
number acted as bearers. The funeral took place at the
cemetery Saturday afternoon at 3pm, leaving his house in
Mariners street at 2.30pm. The paper asked for as many
members of the Beach Companies as possible to please
attend. The above photo shows Roberts coffin being carried
from the church by eight of the thirty lifeboatmen who were
present. His widow – Sarah Ann Hook – died at the family
home at 32 Mariners Street on 18th January 1918 aged 79
and was buried alongside Robert in Lowestoft Cemetery on
23rd January 1918.

The Above headstone has been vandalized as the 3ft tall cross has been kicked off, back in 2015.

CERTIFIED COPY of an ENTRY

Pursuant to the Births and Deaths Registration Act 1953

Registration District _Norfolk_

19 11 . Death in the Sub-district of _Lowestoft_ in the _County of Suffolk_

No.	When and where died	Name and surname	Sex	Age	Occupation	Cause of death	Signature, description, and residence of informant	When registered	Signature of registrar
326	Twenty eighth June 1911 32 Raining Street U.D.	Robert William Hoath	male	63 yard	formerly a Boathouse keeper	Ardeno interosis Heart failure Certified by C. B. Pickende M.R.C.S.	H.E. Goldsmith Present at the death 153 Dickens Street Lowestoft (Park)	Twenty ninth June 1911	C. E. Allerton Registrar

Certified to be a true copy of an entry in a register in my custody.

Superintendent Registrar

04.08.2015 Date

Chapter Seven

Epilogue

The main questions are, what do we learn from Robert's life? What we have to remind us of his and the others sacrifice and how we could keep his sacrifice remembered!

In the Victorian era when Robert was born, grew up and worked it was hard for the working class, if you didn't work you didn't get paid, and you didn't eat, and unlike today there was no welfare state and the only relief open to you was the work house. That was why for the beach-men the cooperative beach companies were so important, and if you had the faster yawl and got to the ships coming in to Lowestoft or in distress first you got the payday. Robert being coxswain had the added benefit of a wage of £80 per year unlike the other crew members who got paid when they turned out, the lifeboat crew was made up from members of all three beach companies so to show no favouritism to one company. I think there's enough evidence to show he didn't once forgo his responsibility to save life in either role as coxswain or as a beach company member, that's why it's amazing there is no acknowledgement of his coxswainship of the Lowestoft lifeboat, it's not like there are not enough rescues to choose from.

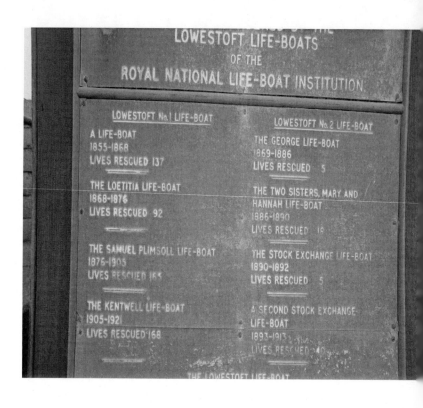

LOWESTOFT LIFE-BOATS
OF THE
ROYAL NATIONAL LIFE-BOAT INSTITUTION

LOWESTOFT No.1 LIFE-BOAT	LOWESTOFT No.2 LIFE-BOAT
A LIFE-BOAT 1855-1868 LIVES RESCUED 137	THE GEORGE LIFE-BOAT 1869-1886 LIVES RESCUED 5
THE LOETITIA LIFE-BOAT 1868-1876 LIVES RESCUED 92	THE TWO SISTERS, MARY AND HANNAH LIFE-BOAT 1886-1890 LIVES RESCUED 18
THE SAMUEL PLIMSOLL LIFE-BOAT 1876-1905 LIVES RESCUED 185	THE STOCK EXCHANGE LIFE-BOAT 1890-1892 LIVES RESCUED 5
THE KENTWELL LIFE-BOAT 1905-1921 LIVES RESCUED 168	A SECOND STOCK EXCHANGE LIFE-BOAT 1893-1913 LIVES RESCUED 40

THE LOWESTOFT LIFE-BOAT

The above plaque is on the side of the present Lifeboat club, but that's it, it would be nice if a simple plaque could be placed down on the ness point, we should be proud of his and the other crew members, and what they achieved.

One of the previous photo's is of Robert's headstone, but what you cannot see is the broken cross behind it, some vandal has kicked it off over the past years, if possible I would like to have it repaired and cleaned up as the lead writing is lifting off.

Please don't forget we have a great resource in Lowestoft, namely the Heritage Centre and the Maritime Museum which contains a wealth of knowledge if you, like me love family history, a visit to the Heritage Centre alone is worth it just to see the model of the beach village.

I really hope you have enjoyed this glimpse into Robert's life and the Victorian time he lived, if you take anything away from this I'm glad he left an impression on you as well.

The End

Many thanks to the Lowestoft Heritage Society with their help in getting Roberts grave restored.